You are the salt of the earth. But if the salt loses its saltiness, how can it be made salty again? It is no longer good for anything, except to be thrown out and trampled by men.

You are the light of the world. A city on a hill cannot be hidden. Neither do people light a lamp and put it under a bowl. Instead they put it on its stand, and it gives light to everyone in the house. In the same way, let your light shine before men, that they may see your good deeds and praise your Father which is in heaven.

JESUS CHRIST

The church must be reminded that it is not the master or the servant of the state, but rather the conscience of the state. It must be the guide and the critic of the state, and never its tool. If the church does not recapture its prophetic zeal, it will become an irrelevant social club without moral or spiritual authority.

MARTIN LUTHER KING, JR.

Endorsements

Dr. Shelley is a pastor who "gets it." He understands that if God's word doesn't apply to the issues of our day and if we are not bold enough to speak to how it applies to those issues, then our faith is dead and it's irrelevant. David has walked the talk. And you'll benefit from walking with him as you read.

David Fowler, President
Family Action Council of Tennessee
Former Tennessee State Senator

"I sought for a man among them... [to] stand in the gap before me for the land..." Ezekiel 22

Christians do not have the luxury of being mere onlookers. We are called to be participants in every area of life, including the public square. Dr. Shelley lays out the challenge and offers the specific guidelines to fulfilling our duty before God and before our fellow men and women to bring Biblical principles into the market place of ideas. If we don't, who will?

Bobbie Patray, President
Tennessee Eagle Forum

Book cover and Eight 32 Publishing logo design:
Ryan Alexander, Emergent Designs www.emergentdesigns.com

Eight 32 Publishing

"Then you will know the truth, and the truth will set you free."
John 8:32
www.Eight32Publishing.com

ISBN – 10: 0615334806
ISBN – 13: 978-0-615-33480-6

Printed in the United States of America

Dedications

I want to dedicate this book to my wife, Jeanna, who made me the happiest man in the world when she married me over twenty years ago. She has faithfully been by my side through school, the various churches I've served and other ministries I've led. She is the most beautiful woman I've ever seen, and the most wonderful friend and confidante a man could ever have.

I also want to dedicate this to my kids: Josh, Melissa and Jacob. The three of you have made your mom and me so proud. You are excellent students, dedicated followers of Christ and a tremendous source of joy to everyone who knows you.

Finally, I'd like to dedicate this book to my parents. Without your love, support and encouragement, I could have never finished all those degrees and written a book. Thank you for your faithfulness to Christ for so many years, and for your example of a loving husband and wife.

Contents

Introduction

What are the two things you don't talk about in polite conversation? Religion and politics. Perhaps the reason that these two topics fall out of the bounds of polite conversation is that they tend to be controversial. Both religion and politics are about truth claims, and truth claims almost always cause disagreement.

A truth claim of religion, for example, is that there is a God and an after-life. For those who disagree on this truth claim, it is hard to have a cordial conversation about religion. When an atheist and a Christian discuss the existence of God and Heaven, blood pressures rise, and emotions run high. There is something within us that wants to convince the other person that we are right and he is wrong. This heightened state of tension is known as a "fight or flight syndrome;" it is an emotional state in which one feels pressure to either fight it out or get away from the conflict. Both want to win the argument, so a breakdown is inevitable. This kind of passionate discourse is just the opposite of the kind of comfortable small talk most people tend to prefer; I think this is especially true for the average Christian.

Politics is another area where truth claims can be divisive, especially within religious circles. Many Christians are uncomfortable talking about political things in church, and they would rather avoid topics that might provoke a heated difference of opinions. Perhaps little can be more stifling to polite conversation in a Sunday School class, for example, than to suddenly discover that a fellow classmate is for abortion when the rest of the class is pro-life.

I've been in church meetings, as perhaps many of you have, where somebody makes a political statement with which most of the group disagrees. There is now a 500-pound gorilla in the room if you know what I mean. You get a sinking feeling in your stomach that from now on you are going to have to listen to this person espouse his or her heretical views every time you come to church. When political arguments come up in church, most Christians will do anything they can to avoid them. And there is an implicit disapproval of the pastor addressing politically controversial topics in church for this very reason: people just don't like being made to feel uncomfortable in church.

"Miss Manners" would probably advise Christians to be courteous when in polite conversation and avoid mixing religion and politics altogether. A polite person will simply choose not to discuss political views if he or she thinks that someone else in the room will robustly disagree, and so we just avoid those topics that tend to divide us. Maybe you've been in a situation among Christian friends, when a person says something like "why can't all those Republicans get off of President Obama's back?" If those around you usually vote Republican, there will be an awkward silence. Or perhaps, you've been in a church service when someone says, "Obama must be the Anti-Christ, and God will use him to judge the sinfulness of America." If the people in the room are mostly Democratic voters, there are going to be some uneasy feelings and strong words to follow. It is easy to understand why political things are considered worldly or inappropriate in church.

I think there is a pervasive notion among Christians in America that because of the "separation of church and state" (and I'll get to that topic later), Christians should just avoid talking about moral or political issues that might cause division within the confines of the church. This is especially true in our nation's pulpits. I've been a preacher for over 20 years, and I've had my share of confrontations with church members who have told me to "just preach the Bible and keep my nose out of politics!" Admittedly, it would be much easier for pastors to just preach on topics like going to Heaven or being blessed by God, and leave out the controversial topics like abortion, racism, homosexuality, gambling, pornography, human trafficking, political and corporate corruption, etc., but America is in a serious place of moral confusion and suffering because the public square is becoming increasingly secular and godless. If Christians don't speak God's truth into the public square, then who will? If Christians abandon political and cultural things, then who will guide the state to make moral decisions? If the truth of God's word is not spoken into law and government, then only the "father of lies," Satan (John 8:44), will be left to tell the politicians what is right and what is wrong.

In large part, there is a spiritual and cultural darkness in America. I'm no electrician, but I have noticed that there isn't a "dark switch" on the wall. There is only a "light switch." Darkness does not dispel the light; rather light dispels darkness. If there is spiritual and moral darkness in this country, and there is, it simply means that the light has been switched off. Of course, Christians know that Jesus tells us (in Matthew 5) that believers are the "light of the world," so if we live in a country of spiritual darkness, AND WE DO, it is high time that the light of the world starts to shine in the culture and in the public square.

Was America ever a Christian Nation?

Before being elected as President of the United States, then-Senator Barack Obama gave a speech saying, "Whatever we once were, we're no longer a Christian nation. At least not just. We are also a Jewish nation, a Muslim nation, and a Buddhist nation, and a Hindu nation, and a nation of nonbelievers."[1] He later reiterated these views while speaking as U.S. President on foreign soil before a predominantly Muslim audience.[2] As I will show in chapter four, it is an historical fact that this country was founded by Christians, on biblical principles, and Christian Scriptures are enshrined in her founding documents.

Through most of her history, America has had a predominantly Christian citizenry whose laws and government were based on biblical principles that reflect a Judeo-Christian sense of justice and morality. Did you know that 29 of the 56 framers of the U.S. Constitution held Bible College or Christian Seminary degrees and that all of them were attendees of Christian churches at some point in their lives?[3] Even in today's multi-cultural, religious pluralism, more than a 75% majority of American citizens still consider themselves Christians in national polls and more than 80% of us say we believe in God.

Proverbs 14:34 declares, "Righteousness exalts a nation, but sin is a reproach (or disgrace) to any people." For several hundred years, Americans (both as colonists of England and later as citizens of the United States) fashioned a system of law and justice that upheld righteousness and punished sin, and they passed these principles on to each succeeding generation through the political and educational processes.

Less than 100 years ago, almost all public school students recited Scripture verses, prayed together in the name of Jesus Christ, and frequently heard visiting preachers who attended the school chapel services. Nearly all courthouses displayed plaques, stone carvings or paintings of the Ten Commandments (just as the U.S. Supreme Court building does today). In those days, behavior defined as sinful in Scripture (i.e. marital infidelity) was punished by law, and the populace held a general agreement of the need for morality and righteousness. State and federal governmental meetings were begun with Scripture reading and prayer, and elected officials regularly quoted passages from the Bible in their political statements. These practices depicted the long history of Christianity in the political life of America. In fact, Alexis de Tocqueville, a French political philosopher who toured the U.S. in the 1830's, wrote:

> "For the Americans, the ideas of Christianity and liberty are so completely mingled that it is almost impossible to get them to conceive of one without the other; it is not a question with them of sterile beliefs bequeathed by the past and vegetating rather than living in the depths of the soul."[4]

Historian Russell Kirk noted of the early American social system, "It was America's moral order, then, that sustained America's social order . . . even though the common man of the West seemed interested chiefly in his own material aggrandizement – still he read his Bible, accepted as good the political framework which he inherited from the Atlantic seaboard and from Britain, and took for granted a moral order that was his custom and his habit."[5]

In the early 21st century, things are quite different. Partly because of political activism on the part of those who would drive all aspects of God out of American life, and partly because of a general apathy and historical ignorance on the part of many people of faith, we now live in a culture where Christian public school teachers are often afraid to have a Bible on their classroom desk, much less read from it, or, God forbid, bow their heads in prayer before eating lunch. Some courts have declared it unconstitutional to have the Ten Commandments displayed on public property, that what the Bible calls sodomy should now be defined as "marriage," that some human life is not considered human life, and that what our grandparents' generation called smut is now constitutionally protected free speech. How did we get this way so quickly?

America is like a great ship in a harbor that has lost the moorings that connected her to the dock. As a result, she is adrift in a sea or moral relativism and social confusion, and this drift is costing her people dearly. Just as the Old Testament prophet lamented the injustice and moral decay of Israel in Isaiah 59:14 - "So justice is driven back, and righteousness stands at a distance; truth has stumbled in the streets, honesty cannot enter" - Americans are facing the same lack of a moral foundation today. Our nation has drifted away from God, and as a result, we are suffering the consequences.

For many years now, I have been a pastor and marriage and family counselor in Southern Baptist churches, mostly serving in Georgia and Tennessee. I also have worked with a number of pro-family, pro-life organizations, as both a volunteer and paid staff member. Currently, I pastor a small church in the city of Nashville, TN, and I also serve as the Vice President of Church and Community Relations for the Family Action Council of Tennessee (www.FACTn.org). FACT is a family policy council associated with Focus on the Family that equips Tennesseans and government officials to promote and defend a culture that values the traditional family for the sake of the common good. FACT promotes public policy that protects the family and recognizes the sanctity of human life, the biblical institution of marriage, traditional moral values, and religious liberty. In my role as Vice President, I seek to identify, educate and mobilize like-minded individuals and churches to stand for righteousness and justice in the public square.

During all these years of ministry, I have witnessed a growing and pervasive moral depravity in American culture and a breakdown of the biblical institution of the family. I'm sure you've noticed it too: perhaps that is why you are reading this book. Some call America a "post-modern" culture, a philosophical term that I don't think very many people understand. I'd call our culture today "post-Christian" and more and more it is becoming even "anti-Christian." Honesty, morality, decency, truthfulness, and responsibility are on the decline, generally speaking, and sin, selfishness, and indifference to God and traditional values seem to be on the rise, especially in the realm of public policy. Along with these problems in our culture, I have seen a serious problem in the modern American church: a general apathy and indifference to the moral state of our society, especially when it comes to involvement in our legal system and political arena.

For some reason, there is an enormous disconnect between the pews and the politicians in this country. Even though we are a nation whose government is "of the people, by the people and for the people," the people are not accurately represented in many governmental decisions. For example, studies have shown for years that most Americans do not practice or condone homosexuality, yet unelected judges (appointed by elected officials) continue to force this issue upon us. They overturn laws that reflect the will of the voters (as in the current battle over Proposition 8 in California) and force government-sanctioned immorality down the throats of a generally moral populace.

More African American babies are killed through abortion than any other ethnicity;[6] in fact, in the United States, the abortion rate for black women is almost five times that for white women.[7] There are significant connections between Planned Parenthood, the nation's largest abortion provider, and the eugenics movement that sought to get rid of the African-Americans after the abolition of slavery.[8] But for some reason, pro-choice President Barack Obama, a strong supporter of Planned Parenthood, garnered nearly 100% of the black vote in 2008.[9] In fact, abortion has killed millions more black people than slavery and the Ku Klux Klan ever did, some 37% of abortions are performed on African American women (who make up only about 3% of the population),[10] and Margaret Sanger and the other founders of Planned Parenthood openly confessed that they desired to see birth control among the African-American people in order to eliminate them over time, yet many prominent black churches openly support pro-abortion politicians.[11] I'm personally thrilled that America has elected a president who is African-American; I just wish that he realized what his policies are doing to decimate African-American children.

What strikes me as most irrational is the fact that the body of Christ could change all of this in one election cycle, but we won't. Elections have consequences, and when Christians don't think biblically about how they vote, they often end up with elected officials who govern in unbiblical ways. Nevertheless, we Christians regularly complain about the moral status of our country.

Is there a Moral Majority in America?

A few decades ago, the late Rev. Jerry Falwell started a movement called "The Moral Majority." He believed, as I do, that most Americans are moral people, and if they could just come together and stand for righteousness and truth, this nation could make a positive turn around. For this belief, Falwell was routinely chastised by the news media as a hate-filled religious bigot, and many in the body of Christ also sought to discredit him for being too political, too fanatical, un-loving, intolerant, etc. Dr. Falwell has gone home to be with the Lord, but he made a lasting impression. There are many other national religious and political leaders who hold to the same hope: Dr. James Dobson, Tom Minnery, Tony Perkins, Ralph Reed, Gary Bauer, Don

Church and State

Wildmon, David Barton, Phyllis Schlafly, Jay Sekulow, Dr. Richard Land, etc. I believe there is a general feeling, among most Americans, that some things are just morally wrong, no matter your partisan preference or religious persuasion, and if we could all just come together and express our values in the ballot box, things would improve in this country.

Consider this example: If a teenage girl becomes pregnant out of wedlock, she can pay five hundred dollars or more in cash and have the baby destroyed at an abortion clinic in Tennessee. Without receiving factual information on the details and medical risks of the procedure and having to think about it for a couple of days, without having to give "informed consent" to the procedure, and without the requirement of doing the procedure in a hospital in case there are complications in the second or third trimester, the girl could have an abortion, go home and die from blood loss or other complications.

When most Christians hear of such a story, there is something within them that cries out, "She is a minor, how could this be?" "Why weren't her parents required to give informed consent?" "Why wasn't this done in a hospital?" Unfortunately, these cries fall on deaf ears because of a state Supreme Court decision handed down by four of five justices in the year 2000. This ruling, *Planned Parenthood of Middle Tennessee vs. Sundquist*, "found" a fundamental right to abortion in the state Constitution of Tennessee. I use quotation marks around the word "found" because there is actually no mention of abortion in the state Constitution of Tennessee. I've read the document word for word many times, and there is absolutely nothing related to abortion in our Constitution. These justices simply "created" this right because of their liberal, unbiblical worldview and desire to legislate from the bench. In order to reverse this decision, the state legislature must pass a constitutional amendment in two consecutive General Assemblies and then place it on the ballot of a gubernatorial election for the people to decide. At a minimum this process takes four years. As of the writing of this book, it has taken nine years so far. With more than fourteen thousand abortions per year in the state, it is unconscionable to think of how many innocent babies have been "legally" slaughtered by this ruling.[12]

Before you get angry with these justices, however, remember how they derived this nearly unquestioned power. For years now, Tennessee has had a plan that allows the Supreme Court justices to be appointed by the Governor, even though Article six, Section three, of the Constitution plainly reads: "The Judges of the Supreme Court shall be elected by the qualified voters of this state." Instead of electing judges like the constitution spells out, we have a plan whereby the governor selects justices for a judicial opening from a panel of candidates presented to him by a selection commission consisting primarily of lobbyists (trial lawyers, the Bar Association, etc.), and his appointments are then "retained" by the voters at the next election. Since it is practically impossible for the average voter to know how these judges have ruled or anything about their worldview, almost all voters elect to retain the judges with little knowledge of the results of these choices. In the 106th Tennessee General Assembly, 2009-2010, conservatives in both parties tried to end this unconstitutional process of selection and retention, but they did not have the votes to return the power of electing judges back to the qualified voters as the constitution requires. Thus, unelected judges, who are unaccountable to the people, continue to legislate from the bench, and the people can do little to nothing about it. Does that make your blood pressure boil? Well, wait just a minute.

Before you get mad at the governor and legislature for maintaining this unconstitutional system, remember that you and I, the voters, put these people in their seats. In the last presidential election, a man was elected Commander in Chief who holds clearly unbiblical views on a number of moral issues. Nevertheless, millions of Christians voted for him because they wanted "change we can believe in" or they thought he could give America "hope." Many simply felt badly about how blacks were treated in the past and thought it was time for a black man to become president. Others voted for him because he is "cool," whatever that means. Nevertheless, in his first year of office, our cool new president has done more to destroy

Church and State

babies in the womb and to legally protect sodomy than any other president in history. Did you know that Mr. Obama, by presidential proclamation, appointed June 2009 the Gay, Lesbian, Bisexual and Transgender month? When the policies of the land and the leadership of the country do not reflect our values and morals, it means that Christian voters have not been paying attention or are not voting at all.

I still think there is a moral majority in this country; by that I mean that most Americans are generally God-fearing, family-loving, law-abiding citizens who work hard, get married, raise children and try to live a good life. I don't for a minute think that all – or even most of these folks – are followers of Jesus Christ in an "evangelical" sense of the word, but I do think they are generally moral and recognize the basic difference between right and wrong. The problem is that our sense of morality does not always translate into how we vote. I recently heard Chuck Colson say: "Culture is religion incarnate," meaning that our religion takes on flesh and blood through the culture. If the culture is sick, that means that the religion of America is sick. That is why I have written this book.

The church can be the salt of the earth and the light of the world in the public square, but we must bring healthy salt and pure light if we want to heal our culture. Perhaps you've often wondered, "Where is the common sense in America? Doesn't anybody know right from wrong anymore?"

Read on …

Section One
Why be Salt and Light

Church and State

Modern Americans stand on the shoulders of giants of the faith, and we are the beneficiaries of a rich history of godly men and women who were salt and light in the public square. Throughout the thousands of years of recorded history, people of faith have shaped the cultural and political worlds in which they lived, quite often at great personal price. In this first section of the book, I will give you a biblical rationale for being involved in the public square and show you some remarkable examples of biblical and historical believers who made a difference for good in their culture because they believed that, "Righteousness exalts a nation, but sin is a disgrace to any people." In the second section, I will give you some practical steps for taking action.

Today, we enjoy so many freedoms that are not free: they were purchased by the blood, sweat and tears of Christians who sacrificed and fought to keep Christian principles alive and well on the face of this earth. Think about Moses the Great Emancipator of the Hebrew slaves. Most people would not think of Moses as a political activist, but he was really the first religious lobbyist in the Bible. Moses lobbied hard for a political outcome, the abolition of Hebrew slavery in Egypt, and he was the trustee of the first written system of laws given by God. The Mosaic system of law, based upon the Ten Commandments, is the cornerstone of practically all just societies throughout the world. Had Moses been under the impression that religious people should stay out politics, law and government, our world would be very different than it is today.

Another emancipator in history was the Christian politician William Wilberforce. Raised in a Christian home of English nobility in the mid-19th century, Wilberforce became incensed at the injustice of the slave trade. Rather than simply look the other way, like so many politicians and clergy of his day, Wilberforce dedicated his entire life to the abolition of slavery in Great Britain, and his example led the way for the abolition of the slave trade in America years later.

Many Christians today falsely think that politics hold no answers. The sentiment is that if Christians would be more spiritual and live out the faith better, the world's social evils would go away. Certainly, we need to do those things, because we must practice what we preach. There is no doubt that much of the blame for the moral landslide in American culture belongs squarely at the feet of Christians who have become so worldly that the morality within the church is no better than without.

But improving the spirituality within the body of Christ is not the only way to redeem the culture outside of the church. Let me ask you a question: Why is it that we don't have slaves today in America like we did 200 years ago? In the early 19th century, slavery was rampant in the southern states, but today nobody owns a slave in the south: Why is that? Is slavery gone because Americans are more spiritual today than they were in the early 1800's? Is slavery gone because we are raising our children better today and helping them embrace the faith of our fathers? Is slavery gone because we are more faithful to our marriage vows than were our ancestors 200 years ago? Is slavery gone today because we pray more or have more people attending our church services than in the early 1800's? Is slavery gone today because we preach the Bible more faithfully than our early American ancestors did? NO.

The only reason slavery is gone today is that the Christians of the 1800's got involved in the political realm and made slavery illegal. Slavery is gone because men like Abraham Lincoln ran for public office and passed the 13th Amendment to the U.S. Constitution that made slavery illegal. If slavery was not illegal today, I guarantee you it would still exist. Think about abortion for a moment. Ripping a baby apart in her mother's womb is just as abhorrent and disgusting a procedure as forcing a man to become a slave, actually it is worse. Yet, abortion is completely legal in the United States of America. Why? Is the reason that America has killed fifty million children through legalized abortion since 1973 due to anything other than the fact that Christians have abandoned the political arena and allowed this atrocity to go on? While we need to pray more, we need to preach the Bible more, we need to teach our children the faith more effectively, we need to be better husbands and wives, we need to witness and evangelize more, etc., we also need to make the killing of a pre-born child illegal, just like our forefathers made slavery illegal. Only when abortion becomes illegal in America, will the slaughter stop.

Unless Christians vote for politicians who will pass laws that outlaw sin, as our forefathers have done throughout history, our nation may not survive. The Old Testament prophet delivered a chilling warning from God that I think the modern American church desperately needs to heed today. I've read a lot of magazines, web sites and books about creative worship, expository and relational preaching, the use of audio/visual technology in church, etc; all in hopes of making a difference in the culture by the way we deliver our message. It's as if we think that the successful church will be the one that is most entertaining and comfortable to the lost.

Some seem to think that the salvation of the American church is wrapped up in using power point and electric guitars, or in filling up stadiums rather than wooden pews, but they are deceived: God doesn't care about how faithfully we preach and how creatively we worship IF we look the other way and ignore injustice. Listen to what God said through the biblical prophet Amos: "I hate, I despise your religious feasts; I cannot stand your assemblies . . . Away with the noise of your songs? I will not listen to the music of your harps. But let justice roll on like a river, righteousness like a never-failing stream!" (Amos 5:21, 23-24). Read what Jesus said about the "institutional church" of his day in the Gospels.

God cares about government and justice, and, as his children, we should too!

Chapter One

We Know We Must Be Engaged

"No candid observer will deny that whatever of good there may be in our American civilization is the product of Christianity. The teachings of the Bible are so interwoven and entwined with our whole civic and social life that it would be literally impossible for us to figure to ourselves what that life would be if these teachings were removed."[13]

PRESIDENT THEODORE ROOSEVELT

Church and State

Despite the widespread notion in the modern American church that Christians should not be involved in political things, I think sincere believers in Christ intuitively know that we cannot abandon this sphere of God's creation. Injustice creates within us a need to see justice done, and that need comes from God the author of justice: there is a moral code written by the Creator on men's hearts. I believe that part of being created in God's image means that we have a sense of right and wrong built into us from birth. It's what Thomas Paine referred to as "common sense."[14] The Apostle Paul referred to it as "the law written on men's hearts,"[15] Aquinas called it "natural law,"[16] Calvin called it the "moral law . . . which God has engraved upon the minds of men,[17] Thomas Jefferson referred to it as the "laws of nature and of nature's God," and I think it exists within all of us.

Let me illustrate what I mean. If an elderly woman is trying to cross a busy street, and a stranger volunteers to walk her across safely, almost all observers would say that the volunteer's behavior is "morally good." You don't have to conduct a million dollar, tax-funded research study to find this out or pass a law to say that helping an old lady across the street is good. It is obvious to most all of us that this is a good thing to do.

On the other hand, if somebody were to walk up to this elderly lady on a busy street and push her under a bus, most would deem the behavior wrong, bad, immoral, sinful, etc. It doesn't take an opinion poll or a referendum to recognize that this behavior is bad: everybody intuitively knows it. This kind of bad behavior is immoral, and it is also illegal. The reason it is illegal is because the moral majority of citizens recognize that such an act is wrong and have made it punishable by law. Some would call this process "legislating morality," i.e. passing laws that condemn immoral, or wrong, behavior as illegal and that is exactly what it is. In fact, laws that punish crime could be said to "legislate morality," but more on that later.

Along with the presence of a natural law on our hearts, there is within us a sense of moral justice that demands satisfaction in such an incident. Almost all of us would say, "Pushing that elderly woman under the bus was wrong, <u>and that man should be punished</u>!" When we hear of a child molester being arrested and punished, we all sense a level of satisfaction that justice has been served. On the contrary, when such a criminal gets off on a technicality and returns to the street, we are all outraged at the judicial inefficiency. This built-in moral desire for justice is within all of us by nature, and I believe it comes from being created in God's image.

The framers of our American government often referred to this built-in sense of morality as "natural law," or the "law of nature's God," and they appealed to it as their rationale for throwing off the tyranny of King George III of England. As the Declaration of Independence highlighted, there are some abuses that must be ceased, even if the written laws of the king, parliament, congress or court do not recognize them as wrong.

Following the opening statement, the Declaration of Independence listed several examples of "repeated injuries and usurpations" by King George. Here, the signers explained that there are some things that are just wrong, even when the king and parliament say that they are right. We know some things to be wrong, intuitively, and Jefferson appealed to this innate sense of morality in his Declaration. "Truths," and the "laws of nature and of nature's God" are "self-evident," he said. You really don't have to explain them to people: we all just sort of know that some things are right and some things are wrong.

University of Texas at Austin Professor J. Budziszewski, a philosopher and ethicist on law and government, has written a fascinating book on this topic called <u>What We Can't Not Know</u>.[18] Budziszewski says, "Even the murderer knows the wrong of murder, the mocker the wrong of mockery, the adulterer the wrong of adultery. He may say that he doesn't, but he does. There are no real moral skeptics; supposed skeptics are playing make-believe, and doing it badly."

There is a natural law that I believe is woven into our very beings by our Creator, and this law guides us into a knowledge of right and wrong. I also believe that most Americans generally live by this internal moral code. Of course, "all have sinned," as Romans 3:23 explains in the Bible, but we all know that sin is wrong, and that is why we need God's salvation. There is a moral majority in America!

What happens too often, however, is that good moral people are easily duped into denying or dismissing the natural impulses of justice and morality within them and somehow convince themselves that it is better to just look the other way when they perceive a wrong being committed. For instance, almost all people would agree that stabbing a tiny baby in the back of the head, sucking out his or her brains with a surgical vacuum, and tossing the lifeless, bloody body in the trash is wrong at the most basic level. If that kind of gruesome murder were deemed to be legal by our Supreme Court for a six-year-old child, there would be a national outrage. Nevertheless, this is precisely what our society has come to view as a legal procedure called abortion. The only difference is that the victim of abortion has yet to be born.

According to various national polls:
- sixty-one percent of Americans say abortion should be illegal after the fetal heartbeat has begun[19] — which occurs in the first month of pregnancy.[20]
- seventy-two percent of Americans say abortion should be illegal after the first 3 months of pregnancy.[21]
- eighty-six percent of Americans say abortion should be illegal after the first 6 months of pregnancy.[22]
- Only sixteen percent of Americans say abortion should be legal at any time for any reason.[23] However, court decisions have made abortion legal throughout all nine months of pregnancy, for any reason.[24]

If it is true that most Americans say the destruction of innocent unborn babies is wrong, why has our nation's highest court called it good (*Roe v. Wade/Doe v. Bolton*), and why have two generations of Americans continued to elect pro-abortion politicians who have kept this behavior legal, and why have we elected "so called" pro-life politicians who have done little or nothing to stop it? The reason, I hate to say, is that sometimes the moral majority is also a silent and weak-willed majority.

When a mugger attacks a defenseless person on a busy city street, most passersby who witness this think, "That's wrong! Somebody should stop him." But what do most passersby do in this situation? Quite often, out of fear or uncertainty, many do nothing at all. Edmund Burke, an influential writer, politician, and philosopher from Ireland in the late 1700's, famously observed, "All that is necessary for the triumph of evil is that good men do nothing." This lack of will to do good, or at least the lack of will to stop evil by good and moral people, creates a vacuum which immoral actions quickly fill. When we consider the impact of the church, universally, we have to be honest and say that while most Christians recognize evil when they see it, we tend to be weak-willed and afraid to take action. As a result, evil actions fill the void, and Christians just look the other way and think, "That's a shame."

In addition to the fact that we are all somewhat weak-willed, I believe that Satan has pulled the wool over the eyes of American Christians in the 20th and 21st centuries by a very clever tactic called "the separation of church and state." This phrase has been uttered, or at least thought, by millions of Christian Americans as they have purposefully looked the other way when our decaying and dark society was crying out for the salt of the earth and the light of the world.

What is the proper role of the church when it comes to matters of the state, i.e. politics, law, and government? If what I have said so far is true, that there is a moral majority in America but we are unwilling to come together and make a difference, then we must ask ourselves, "How do we correct this problem?" My position is that the problem can be corrected, but it will take a sweeping, nation-wide revival of good actions, not just good intentions, on the part of Christians and other moral people. That revival cannot be limited to a change of heart. It must be translated from good intentions to meaningful action in the cultural and political realm. "Did he just say 'political realm?' you ask," Yes. As distasteful to most Christians as the political realm is, Christians cannot abandon politics if we want to be faithful to our calling to be the "salt of the earth" and the "light of the world."

Why are Christians so Reluctant to Get Involved in Politics?

There is a common notion in modern American society that there should be a separation of church and state (usually interpreted that Christians and churches should stay out of the political realm). In my work as a pastor and grass-roots political activist, the most common complaint that I hear from clergy is that they don't want to get involved in anything political because of the "separation of church and state." Usually, those who cry for a separation of church and state mean that the church, and more specifically conservative or evangelical Christians, should keep their noses out of politics. This notion is often claimed to be constitutional, and people of Christian faith frequently state it.

I can remember when the people of my state voted overwhelmingly to amend the state constitution to protect marriage as a "one-man and one-woman" relationship, I heard that the pastor of one large church told his congregation that it is OK to vote for the amendment but he was uncomfortable with it because "you can't legislate morality," and "there should be a separation of church and state." His words summarized what a lot of Christians actually believe about political things. This raises a question: why do so many Christians abhor politics? (By the way, the amendment to establish marriage in Tennessee as being a one-man, one-woman relationship passed by an 81% majority in spite of this pastor's doubts).

I think most religious people don't want anything to do with politics because they have been duped into thinking that it is somehow "wrong" for Christians, especially ministers, to be politically engaged. We see and hear this message constantly in American culture. The television and print news media present a dualism that says, "Christians should help the poor and love people, but stay out of public policy." How often do you see a minister interviewed about a moral/political topic on the evening news? Usually, if a minister is on the evening news, it is because he has done something illegal or immoral. How often do you see ministers come to the state, or national, capitol and proclaim, "thus saith the Lord?" Usually, when a minister comes to the capitol, he is just there to say a nice opening prayer that is pleasant and non-controversial. What kind of prayer do you think the Old Testament prophet Elijah would give at the opening session of Congress today? I'm afraid the church, in general, has bought the lie that she is supposed to stay out of the political realm for at least three reasons:

I. The False Constitutional Separation of Church and State

The First Amendment to the U.S. Constitution plainly forbids the creation of a national church because that would be an "establishment of religion like the Church of England," however; the Constitution says nothing about the so-called "separation of church and state" that is referred to so often in the public discourse today. I know this is going to come as a shock, but the phrase, "separation of church and state," simply does not exist in any our nation's founding documents: the Declaration of Independence and the Constitution (including the Bill of Rights). It is a phrase used by Thomas Jefferson in a personal letter that he wrote to some pastors from the Danbury (CT) Baptist Association of Churches in 1802. The Baptist pastors were concerned about Connecticut establishing a state church that would forbid Baptists from exercising their religious freedom. President Jefferson, commenting on the passage of the First Amendment in a private letter to these Baptist churches, said,

> Believing with you that religion is a matter which lies solely between Man & his God, that he owes account to none other for his faith or his worship, that the legitimate powers of government reach actions only, and not opinions, I

> contemplate with sovereign reverence that act of the whole American people which declared that their legislature should "make no law respecting an establishment of religion, or prohibiting the free exercise thereof," thus building a wall of separation between Church and State (emphasis added).[25]

That's it, folks! That is the only source quoting a "separation of church and state" in early American documents. Jefferson was not writing a Presidential Proclamation, this letter was not part of a Supreme Court ruling, it was not part of some congressional legislation: it was merely one sentence written in a personal letter. If you read the entire letter, it is patently clear that Jefferson meant that such a wall of separation would keep the government out the church's business, and not the other way around. Nevertheless, the idea that the U. S. Constitution guarantees a "separation of church and state" is believed and taught almost universally by our politicians, universities, law schools, news media and even pastors throughout the land.

I do believe that a separation of powers between government and the various institutions of religion is what the Framers of the Constitution had in mind with the First Amendment ("Congress shall make no law respecting the establishment of religion nor prohibiting the free exercise thereof"). They had seen the problems that came with the Church of England being supported by taxes and the clergy being essentially government employees. They were also conscious of the problems of the middle ages in which the Catholic Pope was essentially a king. But the actual words "separation of church and state" are intentionally absent from the Constitution, I think, because it would suggest that the two institutions are not allowed to influence one another at all. In 1985, U.S Supreme Court Chief Justice William Rehnquist spoke out about the nonsense of using Jefferson's separation phrase in legal decisions:

> It is impossible to build sound constitutional doctrine upon a mistaken understanding of constitutional history, but unfortunately the establishment clause has been expressly freighted with Jefferson's misleading metaphor for nearly 40 years. Thomas Jefferson was of course in France at the time

the constitutional amendments known as the Bill of Rights were passed by Congress and ratified by the States. His letter to the Danbury Baptist Association was a short note of courtesy, written 14 years after the amendments were passed by Congress . . . There is simply no historical foundation for the proposition that the framers intended to build the "wall of separation" that was constitutionalized in *Everson* [emphasis added].

Rehnquist continued:

The greatest injury of the "wall" notion is its mischievous diversion of judges from the actual intentions of the drafters of the Bill of Rights. No amount of repetition of historical errors in judicial opinions can make the errors true. The "wall of separation between church and state" is a metaphor based on bad history, a metaphor which has proved useless as a guide to judging. It should be frankly and explicitly abandoned.[26]

So how should we interpret the First Amendment?

If you are wondering how to interpret a sentence written by men who died nearly two hundred years ago, the only sensible thing to do is to read other writings by these same men. From their writings, once can determine what they probably meant by "Congress shall make no law respecting an establishment of religion." In chapter four of this book, I've done exactly that. You will see that the men who framed the Constitution had absolutely no notion of the idea that Christianity and religious principles should be erased from the public square or that we should have a secular, Godless government.

In 1952, President Truman signed into law a joint resolution of Congress to set aside an annual National Day of Prayer, and Congress amended the law in 1988 to establish a more particular date. The law simply reads,

The president shall issue each year a proclamation designating the first Thursday in May as a National Day of Prayer on which

> the people of the United States may turn to God in prayer and
> meditation at churches, in groups and as individuals.

The tradition of designating an official day of prayer actually began with the Continental Congress in 1775, after which President Washington issued a National Day of Thanksgiving Proclamation. Ever since, American presidents have made similar proclamations and "appeals to the Almighty." Historically, all 50 governors, along with presidents, have issued proclamations in honor of the National Day of Prayer.

Nevertheless, a recent ruling by one federal judge has done exactly that: thrown the weight of the federal government behind those who believe in the religion of atheism.

In Madison, Wisconsin, a federal judge ruled April 15 that the statute that sets a day for the National Day of Prayer is unconstitutional, amounting to a governmental call for religious action. The ruling was handed down by U.S. District Court Judge Barbara Crabb.

It is interesting to me that this ruling was handed down by a judge in Madison, WI. The city of Madison, which is also the state capital, is named after James Madison, one of the founders of our country, who, along with Alexander Hamilton, authored The Federalist Papers and laid the foundation for our US Constitution and our Bill of Rights.

James Madison was a Christian who spent over half a century in public service. Madison is often called "The Father of the Constitution." Madison was the youngest delegate to the Continental Congress, a signer of the Declaration of Independence, a member of the Constitutional Convention, a Virginia congressman, the fourth President of the U.S. and the main author of the Bill of Rights.[27]

In an eerily prophetic way, Madison must have known that one day Americans might question the constitutionality of the Ten Commandments displays, National Days of Prayer, and other Christian symbols in the public square. He wrote,

> We have staked the whole future of American civilization, not
> upon the power of government, far from it. We have staked

the future of all our political institutions upon the capacity of each and all of us to govern ourselves, to control ourselves, to sustain ourselves <u>according to the Ten Commandments of God</u> (emphasis added).[28]

Psalm 33:11 says, "Blessed is the nation who's God is the Lord." This verse implies two things: 1. that nations have a god, and 2. that a nation had better get it right. You see, all nations have a god. It may be the Judeo-Christian God of the Bible or it may be Allah or the Hindu gods, etc., or it may the secular humanist god of man, but all nations worship something and appeal to some greater source of wisdom and morality. The question is, what God is America's God? We had better get it right! In 1854, The U.S. Congress had it right, declaring:

> Had the people, during the Revolution, had a suspicion of any attempt to war against Christianity, that Revolution would have been strangled in its cradle ... In this age, there can be no substitute for Christianity ... That was the religion of the founders of the republic and they expected it to remain the religion of their descendants.[29]

When the Capitol building was completed in 1800, Christian worship services were held each Sunday morning in the Hall of the House. Then-President Jefferson not only attended the Sunday services on a regular basis, but he ordered the Marine Band to play in the services. Jefferson also began church services in the War Department building and the Treasury building allowing Americans a choice of places to worship in Washington D.C. if they wished, and by 1853, the church at the Capitol was the largest congregation in America with some 2,000 worshippers in attendance on any given Sunday. Jefferson also urged local governments to make land available for Christian purposes. He provided federal funding for missions work among the Native American tribes and declared that religious schools should receive the patronage of the government.

On the Jefferson memorial, in Washington D.C., one finds these words engraved:

Church and State

"God who gave us life, gave us liberty at the same time. Can the liberties of a nation be secure when we have removed their only sure basis, a conviction in the midst of the people that those liberties are the gifts of God?"

Does that statement sound like someone who did not believe in the importance of Christian values being preserved through government?

During the arduous debates of the Constitutional Convention, the delegates were hopelessly gridlocked on how to proceed, and some of the delegates were ready to give up the entire process and go home without forming a federal government.

Ben Franklin, was present throughout the process, though being in his eighties, he had not said very much. Franklin is another founding father that historical revisionists like to paint as a non-Christian, but listen to what actually happened. Franklin wisely observed:

> In this situation of this Assembly, groping as it were in the dark to find political truth, and scarce able to distinguish it when presented to us, how has it happened, Sir, that we have not hitherto once thought of humbly applying to the Father of lights to illuminate our understandings?
>
> In the beginning of the Contest with G. Britain, when we were sensible of danger we had daily prayer in this room for the divine protection. "Our prayers, Sir, were heard, and they were graciously answered. All of us who were engaged in the struggle must have observed frequent instances of a Superintending providence in our favor. To that kind providence we owe this happy opportunity of consulting in peace on the means of establishing our future national felicity.
>
> And have we now forgotten that powerful friend? I have lived, Sir, a long time, and the longer I live, the more convincing proofs I see of this truth- that God governs in the affairs of men. And if a sparrow cannot fall to the ground without his notice, is it probable that an empire can rise without his aid?
>
> We have been assured, Sir, in the sacred writings, that "except the Lord build the House they labour in vain that build it." I firmly believe this; and I also believe that without his concurring aid we shall

succeed in this political building no better than the Builders of Babel: We shall be divided by our little partial local interests; our projects will be confounded, and we ourselves shall become a reproach and bye word down to future ages. And what is worse, mankind may hereafter from this unfortunate instance, despair of establishing Governments be Human Wisdom and leave it to chance, war and conquest.

I therefore beg leave to move, that henceforth prayers imploring the assistance of Heaven, and its blessings on our deliberations, be held in this Assembly every morning before we proceed to business, and that one or more of the Clergy of the City be requested to officiate in that service.

The delegates then elected to take a three-day break from their work, and they proceeded to go across the street to pray and worship together in church. When they came back, they sat down and wrote the longest lasting constitution on the face of the earth. Does that sound like a group of men who think it is unconstitutional to proclaim a National Day of Prayer?

II. Fear of the Internal Revenue Service

Another reason that Christian ministers have surrendered the political arena to the non-religious is a fear of being audited by the Internal Revenue Service. Pastors are afraid that if they speak out too strongly their church's tax-free status will be revoked. Actually, pastors have nothing to fear but fear itself. The Alliance Defense Fund points out:

Historically, churches have emphatically, and with great passion, spoken Scriptural truth from the pulpit about government and culture. Historians have stated that America owes its independence in great degree to the moral force of the pulpit. Pastors have proclaimed Scriptural truth throughout history on great moral issues such as slavery, women's suffrage, child labor and prostitution. Pastors have also spoken from the pulpit with great frequency for and against the election of the various candidates for government office.

All that changed in 1954 with the passage of the "Johnson amendment" which restricted the right of churches and pastors to speak Scriptural truth about candidates for office. The Johnson amendment was proposed by then-Senator Lyndon Johnson, and it changed the Internal Revenue Code to prohibit churches and other non-profit organizations from supporting or opposing a candidate for office. After the Johnson amendment passed, churches faced a choice of either continuing their tradition of speaking out or silencing themselves in order to retain their church's tax exemption. The Internal Revenue Service, in conjunction with radical organizations like Americans United for Separation of Church and State, have used the Johnson amendment to create an atmosphere of intimidation and fear for any church that dares to speak Scriptural truth about candidates for office or issues.[30]

I travel around the state of Tennessee speaking before gatherings of clergy and meeting with them one on one. I don't think I've ever met a pastor who was not aware of the I.R.S. regulations against endorsing candidates in the pulpit. It is probably one of the most commonly understood church-related legal rulings. The IRS.gov web site says:

> Under the Internal Revenue Code, all section 501(c)(3) organizations are absolutely prohibited from directly or indirectly participating in, or intervening in, any political campaign on behalf of (or in opposition to) any candidate for elective public office. Contributions to political campaign funds or public statements of position (verbal or written) made on behalf of the organization in favor of or in opposition to any candidate for public office clearly violate the prohibition against political campaign activity. Violating this prohibition may result in denial or revocation of tax-exempt status and the imposition of certain excise taxes.

> Certain activities or expenditures may not be prohibited depending on the facts and circumstances. For example, certain voter education activities (including presenting public forums and publishing voter education guides) conducted in a non-partisan manner do not constitute prohibited political campaign activity. In

addition, other activities intended to encourage people to participate in the electoral process, such as voter registration and get-out-the-vote drives, would not be prohibited political campaign activity if conducted in a non-partisan manner.

On the other hand, voter education or registration activities with evidence of bias that (a) would favor one candidate over another; (b) oppose a candidate in some manner; or (c) have the effect of favoring a candidate or group of candidates, will constitute prohibited participation or intervention.

The Internal Revenue Service provides resources to exempt organizations and the public to help them understand the prohibition. As part of its examination program, the IRS also monitors whether organizations are complying with the prohibition.[31]

Wow! Whatever happened to the freedom of speech and the freedom of religion? Didn't anybody read the Bill of Rights before voting for this in Congress?

You would think that since the Johnson Amendment's passage in 1954, thousands of churches would have been investigated by the IRS over violation of this law. After all, so many politicians speak in churches during election campaigns (I remember seeing the Clintons preaching in churches on television); surely those churches have had their tax-exempt status removed or at least threatened. You might think that the IRS is constantly revoking the tax-exempt status of churches all over America because they simply refuse to be silenced.

Guess how many churches in the U.S. have had their tax-exempt status permanently revoked by the IRS since 1954:

ZERO!

That's right, not one single church has permanently lost its tax-exempt status for political speech. Only one church has even had its tax-exempt status temporarily removed for advocating against a candidate in an election. The Church at Pierce Creek in Binghamton, New York, was investigated by the IRS about their full-page newspaper ads (in *USA Today* and *The Washington Times*) encouraging people to vote against then Gov. Bill Clinton for president back in 1992 because of his positions on abortion and homosexuality. These ads also solicited "tax-deductible donations" to defray the cost of the ad, and people responded by giving to the church for that purpose, which compounded the problem. The IRS only revoked the church's tax-exempt status after negotiations broke down with the church. Later, the church filed a lawsuit and regained their tax-exempt status under the law.[32] No other church in America has lost its tax-exempt status over political activity!

Nevertheless, churches and pastors all across this nation still think that if they preach on political and cultural issues, from a biblical perspective, they might get investigated by the I.R.S. and have their tax-exempt status removed. In 2008, the Alliance Defense Fund, a premier national legal group that defends the constitutional rights of Christians, organized a concerted effort to push back against this unconstitutional government intrusion. On September 28, 2008, numerous pastors participated in "Pulpit Freedom Sunday" by preaching a sermon specifically addressing the candidates running for president in light of scriptural truths. I preached a sermon based on a version of this book at my church on September 27, 2009, the second annual observance.

There really is no reason for our churches to be silent. For example, during the presidential primaries in May 2008, the Rev. Gus Booth of Warroad Community Church in Minnesota told his congregation: "If you are a Christian, you cannot support a candidate like Barack Obama or Hillary Clinton for president . . . they both support abortion and homosexual marriage, and the Scripture vehemently opposes both." Months later, Pastor Booth preached another sermon addressing the 2008 presidential election. He then turned himself in to the I.R.S., sending them a copy of both sermons. The I.R.S. notified Pastor Booth that it would take no action against him or the church.[33]

The 1954 Johnson Amendment is unconstitutional and should be challenged in court for the following reasons:

1. It is a violation of the *Free Exercise* clause of the First Amendment: "Congress shall make no law respecting the establishment of religion, nor prohibiting the free exercise thereof or abridging the freedom of speech, or of the press; or the right of the people peaceably to assemble, and to petition the Government for a redress of grievances." Congress, and subsequently the IRS or any other government entity, has no business monitoring or regulating or prohibiting what is communicated by a church. This prohibition substantially burdens the religious expression of a congregation and its clergy.

2. It is a violation of the *Free Speech* clause of the First Amendment. The government has no business deciding what clergy can and cannot say from their pulpits.[34]

Hopefully, one day, Christians will stand up to the IRS and abolish this unconstitutional policy. Hopefully, one day, Christians will stand up to the abortion industry and strike down *Roe v. Wade* and *Doe v. Bolton* too...hopefully.

III. Perception that Politics is about Partisan Power

A third reason that religious people tend to shy away from political engagement, in my mind, is that they perceive politics to be about worldly partisan power, and Christians are trained to think in terms of other-worldly or spiritual power. When Christians get engaged in politics, it is usually a reaction to some alarming political scandal, and believers become outraged as a knee-jerk reaction. For instance, when a decades-old monument of the Ten Commandments is threatened by the A.C.L.U. some churches will get involved and speak out. If the local school board votes to ban a student-led Bible study from the schools, everybody gets up in arms and makes a big fuss. Many of the Christians who speak out against such actions would have to confess that they had never done anything like that before.

Christians like to think that as long as they read their Bibles, pray, love their kids, and are active church members, the social and moral problems of society will somehow go away. Christians are generally pacifists, and I include myself in that categorization. We don't like to argue, for the most part, and we hope that the problems will go away without having to confront the other side. Underneath all of this, Christians have a hope that Christ will soon return, and all of these moral issues will be corrected by God. Nevertheless, as Christians further disengage from the public square, through apathy or faulty theology, the world continues to become more and more sinful and anti-Christian.

When the U.S. Supreme Court first began examining embryonic stem cell research in the 1990's, a process in which human beings are created in test tubes and then destroyed as part of a scientific experiment.[35] The famous movie star, Christopher Reeve, said: "When matters of public policy are debated, no religion should have a seat at the table."[36] How can you argue with Superman? The other day, I heard a radio interview with a huge 1980's rock star. He was arguing that morality is merely religion and that religion is bad because it tells people what they can and cannot do. A lot of non-religious people bristle at the idea of religious people telling them that their personal choices are wrong. These kind of statements reflect a worldview that since the 1950's has been widely circulated in the entertainment industry, in the news media, in the schools and colleges, in the courts and legislatures: *churches should keep their noses out of the culture and out of politics!* This is a tragedy, but the greatest tragedy is that this false idea has been swallowed by the American church.

Colossians 2:8 warns: "See to it that no one takes you captive through hollow and deceptive philosophy, which depends on human tradition and the basic principles of this world rather than on Christ." I'm afraid that is exactly what has happened to the church in America.

We have been taken captive by the hollow and deceptive philosophy of the "separation of church and state," and this worldly principle has largely sidelined the body of Christ from being engaged in the public square.

If the devil was the offensive coordinator a football team, and the church was the opposing defense, his most effective play would be to somehow convince the defense to get off the field and stand on the sidelines. Then his evil forces would have a clear, easy run to the goal line. If the church doesn't say "Right is right and wrong is wrong," then who will? Hollywood? The A.C.L.U? The gambling industry? The illegal drug industry? The prostitution industry?

I've been a Christian almost all of my life, and I have studied the Bible in its' original languages for two decades. I have written a sermon on every book of the Bible and just about every significant topic that the Bible addresses. During my years of formal education, especially during the eight long years of my Ph.D. in theology, I read hundreds of books on theology, political science, philosophy, church history, American history, and the role that Christians have played in the governmental process. What I have concluded from those years of study is that God clearly commands his children to be involved in the political process as the salt of the earth and the light of the world. Contrary to public opinion in modern-day America, Christians should, <u>in fact we must, stick our noses into politics, law and government!</u> If God cares about justice and righteousness, then his followers should too.

In Matthew 5:13-16, Jesus talked about two analogies of the church, salt and light, and he explained what would happen if the "salt lost its saltiness" or the light was "hidden under a bowl."

> *You are the salt of the earth. But if the salt loses its saltiness, how can it be made salty again? It is no longer good for anything, except to be thrown out and trampled by men. You are the light of the world. A city on a hill cannot be hidden. Neither do people light a lamp and put it under a bowl. Instead they put it on its stand, and it gives light to everyone in the*

house. In the same way, let your light shine before men, that
they may see your good deeds and praise your Father in
heaven.

We usually think of this passage in the context of evangelism and missions, but it really applies to all areas of life. The Great Commission of Christ (Matthew 28:18-20) says that we are to make disciples of <u>all the world</u>. Churches have done a pretty good job of sending missionaries to the "uttermost parts of the earth." Most churches give money to local missions and support ministries to the inner cities, they feed the hungry, clothe the naked, provide medicine for the sick, evangelize the youth, care for the elderly, etc. All of that is wonderful, but let me ask this question: Does God not also care about those who govern our nation? Do we really think that God doesn't care about law and politics? Does the commandment to make disciples stop at the doorstep of the capitol or the White House or the courthouse? Does the Great Commission read "Go, therefore, into all the world and make disciples. . .*except stay out of the capitol building because there's supposed to a separation of church and state?*" No, the Bible clearly teaches that Christians are commanded to bring the Gospel, and the truth of Scripture, into the public square as well as every other area of the world.

Abraham Kuyper was a rare bird: a Christian pastor and Prime Minister of the Netherlands. He declared, "There is not a square inch in the whole domain of our human existence over which Christ, who is Sovereign over all, does not cry: 'Mine!'"[37] Just as Christ is sovereign Lord over the realm of the church, the home and the family, He is sovereign Lord over the realm of state. In fact, the Bible teaches us that God created three institutions in this world: the family (Genesis), the church (Acts) and the state (Exodus). We don't usually have a problem educating people on what God says and thinks about the family or about the church. Yet, as I try to speak in churches and address various ministerial gatherings, I find a great ignorance, on the part of Christians, about what God says and thinks about the state.

For the Christian, Politics is about Stewardship

Writing for the Family Research Council, one Washington D.C. pastor said, "Either God matters or He doesn't. His Truth guides and infuses every aspect of our lives - or it is irrelevant, and nothing but pretty poetry and impossible standards. I believe He matters. I believe His Truth covers all. I believe the church is about politics at least as much as it is about potlucks. I believe, in our hearts, our people know this." [emphasis added].[38] Romans 13:1 says: "Everyone must submit himself to the governing authorities, for there is no authority except that which God has established. The authorities that exist have been established by God." If God is the creator of all authority, then He is Lord over all authority, and that includes the political process. As stewards of God's creation, we must also be stewards of the political process.

When the salt and light are not present in the political arena, bad things can happen. On the other hand, when Christians do bring salt and light into the public policy arena, good things can happen. A nation that is governed by righteous people, who are accountable not only to the voters but accountable to God himself, will be a nation that is blessed by God.

The Tennessee Constitution (1870, Article IX, Section 2) states, "No person who denies the being of God or a future state of rewards and punishments shall hold any office in the civil department of this state." The New Hampshire Constitution (1784, Article VI of the Bill of Rights) reads: "Morality and piety, rightly grounded on evangelical principles, would give the best and greatest security to government" and "that the knowledge of these [morality and piety] was most likely to be propagated by the institution of the public worship of the Deity, and public instruction in morality and religion." The Constitution of Delaware (1776, Article XXII) required that all those elected to public office declare: "I do profess faith in God the Father, and in Jesus Christ the Son, and the Holy Ghost, one God, blessed forevermore; and I acknowledge the Holy Scriptures of the Old and New Testaments to be given by divine inspiration." The Constitution of Georgia (1777, Article VI) required every member of the House of Assembly "shall be of the Protestant religion," and the Constitution of Massachusetts (1780, Article III of the Bill of Rights) said: "the Legislature shall from time to time authorize and require the several towns, parishes, precincts, and other bodies politic, or religious societies, to make suitable provision, at their own expense, for the institution of the public worship of God, and for the support and maintenance of public Protestant teachers of piety, religion, and morality, in all cases where such provision shall not be made voluntarily" (there's a fascinating list of statements regarding religious liberty from the various state constitutions in the Appendix of this book).

When the words God or religion were used in the 17th and 18th centuries of America, it was always a reference to the Christian religion. Why did the framers of all fifty state constitutions feel that it was essential for citizens to embrace the Christian faith and that only God-fearing people serve in public office? I think it was because they understood that when a leader only fears losing his elected office, and does not fear God, he or she might do anything it takes in order to stay in power. In other words, if there is no authority greater than that of the majority of voters, then "might makes right." When you take God out of the picture, along with his eternal laws and standards of truth and morality, then the side with the most votes, or the most bullets, gets to decide what is right and what is wrong. If the church does not speak out for truth and righteousness, then the devil certainly will. Then evil will be called good, and good will be called evil.

Christians must understand that all authority belongs to God and is delegated to us. As Romans 13 explains, the magistrate, or ruler, is the *diakonos* (Greek), or servant/minister, of God. The authority that the ruler holds is actually God's authority, and God has delegated that authority to him for the good of the people. Even what we do in the ballot box, by casting a vote for a candidate or an ordinance, proposition or amendment, is exercising our God-given, delegated authority. Therefore, we are stewards of that authority and must exercise it as such. Politics, for the believer, should not be about gaining power or beating the other candidate or party; it should be about good stewardship of God's delegated authority.

In Matthew 25, Jesus gave us the parable of the talents. In the story, a wealthy landowner was leaving for a long trip, so he called three of his servants together and gave each of them a "talent." The talent can represent almost anything: money, ability, etc. As the story goes, two of the servants displayed good stewardship of what they had been given. They used their gifts and multiplied them. The other servant, out of fear, buried his talent in the ground. When the master returned to settle his accounts, he praised and rewarded the good stewardship of the first two servants, but he scolded the laziness of the third. As punishment, the master took away the talent that had been entrusted to the "lazy, wicked servant," and sent him away.

Consider: What if one talent, with which we Americans have been entrusted, is the ability to elect those who rule over us? If we think of the vote as a talent, I ask you, "How have we, as American Christians, stewarded our voting?" Have we been faithful stewards of the delegated power of the vote by examining the candidates and voting for those who share our biblical values, or have we mismanaged the talent by voting for those who look good on the outside, but have no biblical and moral guidance on the inside? What is worse: have we been lazy and wicked with our talent by burying it in the ground, i.e. not even being registered to vote? If so, should we be surprised if one day we have the right to vote taken away from us all together?

In the 2008 Presidential elections, 130 million Americans voted, but 76 million eligible voters did not.[39] There are an estimated 60 million evangelical Christians in this country, yet in the 2000 presidential election, some 45 million Christians did not vote.[40] In this election, a president was elected who, for the first time in our history, has declared a month "Gay, Lesbian, Bisexual and Transgender month" and Mr. Obama has advanced taxpayer funding of abortion more than any other. Mr. Obama says that he is a Christian, but since moving to Washington D.C., the Obamas attended church only a few times since inauguration. While Mr. Obama all but ignored the annual National

Day of Prayer in 2009, he went to great lengths to commemorate the Muslim holiday, Ramadan. Yet, millions of Christians voted for this man, assuming he is a good Christian politician. I love the fact that America has elected a black man as president, but remember it was Dr. Martin Luther King, Jr., who told us to judge a man, not by the color of his skin, but by the content of his character.

Rev. Charles Finney, a powerful preacher who was responsible for thousands coming to Christ through revival meetings in the early years of our republic, wrote these convicting words:

> The Church must take right ground in regard to politics . . . . [T]he time has come that Christians must vote for honest men and take consistent ground in politics. . . . Christians have been exceedingly guilty in this matter. But the time has come when they must act differently . . . . God cannot sustain this free and blessed country which we love and pray for unless the Church will take right ground . . . . It seems sometimes as if the foundations of the nation are becoming rotten, and Christians seem to act as if they think God does not see what they do in politics. But I tell you He does see it, and He will bless or curse this nation according to the course [Christians] take [in politics].[41]

This was written in 1830! How much more do we need to heed these words today? For the Christian, politics is not about acquiring worldly power or about Republicans and Democrats beating the other side. For the Christian, politics is really about the obedience to the cultural mandate of Jesus in Matthew 5:13-16: it is about being the salt of the earth and light of the world. It is about standing up for righteousness and justice and calling a sin, a sin.

The African American minister, statesman and abolitionist of the 1800's, Rev. Frederick Douglas said, "I have one great political idea. That idea is an old one. It is widely and generally assented to, nevertheless, it is very generally trampled upon and disregarded. The best expression of it, I have found in the Bible, 'Righteousness exalts a nation, but sin is a reproach to any people.' This constitutes my politics; the negative and positive of my politics, and the whole of my politics. I feel it my duty to do all in my power to infuse this idea into the public mind."[42] Amen, Brother Douglas! That is my life's purpose too, and it is the reason I have written this book.

God's people, the church, must be engaged in the political arena so that our nation can become a righteous nation once again. We cannot continue to ignore the sin in our culture and political system for it is a reproach to our people. The salt has lost its savor and the light is hidden under a bowl. America, we must wake up before it is too late!

Chapter Two

The Church is Separated from the State

"We are a Christian nation, deeply conscious that the foundation of all liberty is religious faith."[43]

PRESIDENT DWIGHT D. EISENHOWER

The *Tennessean* newspaper (March 4, 2009) ran a front-page story entitled, "God Cover-up Puts Schools Back in court." The story involved a public school in Wilson County, TN, where school officials covered over the words "Pray with us" on a poster that a student created and hung on the wall in the school. The poster was promoting a student-led prayer event on the campus called "See You at the Pole." This is a nation-wide event that students participate in each year as school gets underway. The students gather at the school flagpole, before the school day begins, and pray for their school and for their country. The court case involving the Lakeview Elementary School (Mt. Juliet) alleged that school officials refused to allow the posters, which were all hand-made by students of the school, to use the words "Pray with us," "God bless the USA," and "In God we trust." These phrases were censored in a public school, even though "In God we trust," is our national motto and is printed on every piece of currency produced in the United States of America.

Mt. Juliet, Tennessee, not far from where I live, is a community that is filled with churches and religious people who believe in prayer. I would guess that many, if not most, of the teachers and administrators at this school consider themselves to be Christians and attend church on a regular basis. So why was this action taken to infringe the religious freedom of these students?

The school board of Wilson County was sued in 2006 by the American Civil Liberties Union (ACLU) for allowing a group of praying parents to meet on the school campus and pass out notes to students saying that they were praying for them – *what a crime!* According to ACLU-Tennessee staff,

> It is unfortunate that we had to go to Court to protect religious freedom but we had no other choice. We are pursuing this lawsuit in order to ensure *the constitutional guarantee of separation of church and state* so that Wilson County residents can decide for themselves whether or not they want to practice a particular religious faith (emphasis added).

Church and State

There are two false assumptions in this statement: One is that the actions of the ACLU protect religious freedom, and the other is that there is a "constitutional guarantee of separation of church and state." I'll cover both of those issues in greater depth in a moment. Fortunately, the Alliance Defense Fund fought back against the ACLU, and they won. But after all of that, it is no wonder the leaders of this school were scared to death of any more religious controversies on the school campus in 2008.

You might not realize that the ACLU has highly paid lawyers who lobby our state legislatures every day. In fact, you probably did not know that in June of 2008 the ACLU launched the largest fundraising campaign in its 88-year history. The campaign's goal of raising $335 million has been helped significantly by a $12 million contribution from atheist billionaire, George Soros. There's an old saying, "what you don't know can't hurt you," but it is patently false. What you don't know can hurt you. Well, what you probably don't know, and what is most frightening about this new effort, is that the ACLU said: "targets for expansion include Michigan, Missouri, Mississippi, Montana, New Mexico and Tennessee."[44] These states, traditionally thought of as conservative, family-friendly states, are being targeted by the ACLU. Why? Perhaps it is because the body of Christ is too ignorant and apathetic to present any opposition.

I recently wrote an article for my denominational newspaper about the success of a constitutional amendment in Tennessee to reverse a state Supreme Court ruling that deregulated abortion in this state. To me, the passage of the amendment was a great victory and reason for praise to God, but not everyone saw this the same way. One pastor wrote me and said, "Why should we praise God that a woman's right to choose might be taken away? Don't you know there is a separation of church and state in this country?" Coming from a pastor, this comment explains a lot about the ignorance of many church members.

The origin of the "Separation of Church and State"

In a public letter from the American Family Association and the Family Research Council, U. S. Senator Jim DeMint (R-South Carolina) wrote the following summary on the silence of churches in the public square:

> Dear Pastors and Religious Leaders:
> The long debate over the "separation of church and state" has convinced many religious leaders that their opinions are not welcome in political debates. Many pastors hesitate to explain that government policies have helped cause the decline of America's culture, morality and spirituality. Many people of faith have given up their freedom of speech and the freedom to practice their religious principles in all areas of their lives. I am writing you today to remind you that religious principles and biblical teachings produced the values and policies that made America exceptional, prosperous, and good.[45]

I think Sen. DeMint's observations succinctly highlight the real reason for the moral downslide in America: the churches, and primarily the pulpits of the churches, have been silent when they needed to speak out on political and cultural matters. Christians have bought the lie that there is a constitutional "separation of church and state," (interpreted to mean that pastors can't preach about political things) and this deception has silenced the only element of society that would speak into culture the truth of God's word. If you want to win a football game at all costs, you injure all of the offensive linemen so that your team can attack the quarterback. Satan knows that if he can sideline the church, there is nothing left to stop him from destroying the culture. As Dr. Martin Luther King, Jr., wrote:

> The church must be reminded that it is not the master or the servant of the state, but rather the conscience of the state. It must be the guide and the critic of the state, and never its tool.

> If the church does not recapture its prophetic zeal, it will become an irrelevant social club without moral or spiritual authority.[46]

King was right about the role of the church, and his words not only apply to the issue of racial injustice. In my estimation, many American churches are little more than "irrelevant social clubs without moral or spiritual authority." We preachers are too concerned about building our own earthly kingdoms (i.e. bigger buildings and larger crowds) to risk losing members and offending visitors by preaching the truth of God's word. If the church doesn't tell society that pornography is wrong, then who will? Hugh Heffner? If the church doesn't declare the sanctity of human life then who will? Planned Parenthood? If the church doesn't declare, "Thus saith the Lord," then who will?

As I mentioned in the previous chapter, the First Amendment to the U.S. Constitution plainly forbids the creation of a national church, because that would be an "establishment of religion," however, the Constitution says nothing about the so-called "separation of church and state" that is referred to so often in the public discourse today. The phrase, "separation of church and state," simply does not exist in any our nation's founding documents: the Declaration of Independence and the Constitution (including the Bill of Rights). It is a phrase used by Thomas Jefferson in a personal letter that he wrote to some pastors from the Danbury (CT) Baptist Association of Churches in 1802 (see text of the letter in the Appendix to this book).

In the early 1800's, many of the original states had churches sanctioned by state governments. These were "established churches," and because they were state matters, they were not forbidden in the U.S. Constitution. The First Amendment only prohibited the U. S. Congress from establishing a federal religion; it said nothing to the states.[47] Mostly, the state churches were Anglican, Congregational, or Presbyterian. This was so due to the will of the majority as each state church was created through their elected representatives. The only state without an official church was Rhode Island. R.I. had been settled by a Baptist, Roger Williams, and was uninvolved in the Constitutional Convention.

James Madison, a signer of the Declaration of Independence, a Framer of the Constitution, and the author of the Virginia Declaration of Rights (1776), helped fashion the First Amendment. To address the concerns that the Bill of Rights might hinder the continuance of state churches, Madison explained that: "The civil rights of none shall be abridged on account of religious belief or worship, nor shall any national religion be established, nor shall the full and equal rights of conscience be in any manner, or on any pretest, abridged."

For hundreds of years before the creation of the U.S. Constitution in 1789, America functioned quite satisfactorily without any great commotion over the issue of church and state separation. The Christian religion, in some form or fashion, was held by all of the signers of the Declaration of Independence and the Framers of the Constitution. Their own writings prove this, and author David Barton has shown that even the two "least Christian" of these men, Thomas Jefferson and Ben Franklin, were far more religious than what we would describe today as members of the "Religious Right."[48] John Quincy Adams, the sixth president of the U.S., said:

> Our political way of life is by the Laws of Nature and of Nature's God, and of course presupposes the existence of God, the moral ruler of the universe, and a rule of right and wrong, of just and unjust, binding upon man, preceding all institutions of human society and government.[49]

Presidents George Washington, John Adams, and James Madison, with Congress' approval, issued Thanksgiving Day proclamations, and Presidents James Munroe, John Quincy Adams, Andrew Jackson, and Martin Van Buren, with Senate approval, proposed and signed Indian treaties that provided for the government to support various Christian religious needs of the Native Americans. There were numerous Indian treaties that used federal tax dollars to provide Christian ministries to the Native American communities.[50]

Church and State

The early American culture was almost exclusively Christian (this is surmised from the literary publications of the period), and all of the early American presidents made public declarations to their faith in Christ. Most of the federal buildings and monuments in Washington, D. C. have religious statements and biblical passages inscribed in stone, our Congress is led each day in prayer, our Supreme Court begins each session with the statement, "God save this honorable court," and our religious freedoms are the envy of the world.

Christianity has always been understood as the bedrock of our system of laws and government. In 1830, the visiting French political philosopher, Alexis De Tocqueville, commented:

> I do not know whether all Americans have a sincere faith in their religion – for who can search the human heart? – but I am certain that they hold it to be indispensable to the maintenance of republican institutions. This opinion is not peculiar to a class of citizens or to a party, but it belongs to the whole nation and to every rank of society.[51]

Furthermore, he said:

> There is no country in the whole world in which the Christian religion retains a greater influence over the souls of men than in America – and there can be no greater proof of its utility, and of its conformity to human nature, than that its influence is most powerfully felt over the most enlightened and free nation of the earth.[52]

How Times Have Changed

In the early 21st century, the biblical bedrock of American government is crumbling due to a pervasive lie that the Constitution requires the church (the body of Christ) to stay out of matters of the state. This doctrine has given the church a rationale to be silent on cultural and political issues, and the nation is morally ignorant because of it. Only one-third of U.S. adults consider themselves to be "mostly conservative" on social and political matters, and about half as many (17 percent) say they are "mostly liberal" on such matters. [53] This means that the majority of American adults have no real preferences on social and political matters. Is it any wonder that we are suffering in so many areas of society? Over fifty million babies have died in America through legalized abortion, the equivalent of the population of several states, and most Christian people either do not know about this infanticide or do not really care. The OT prophet Hosea lamented, "My people are destroyed for lack of knowledge." [54]

Many Christian Americans today would tell you that the words, "separation of church and state" are written in the Constitution, even though they are not, because millions of Americans are historically, and biblically, ignorant. Jefferson gets the blame for introducing the separation doctrine, but actually it was Supreme Court Justice Hugo Black that moved the separation phrase into common jurisprudence in the 1947 decision, *Everson v. Board of Education*.

As a publicly acknowledged Klansman, Justice Black surely must have agreed with the Klan's oath of allegiance, to "most zealously ... shield and preserve ... (the) separation of church and state." [55] Alan Sears, of the Alliance Defense Fund, says, "Klan doctrine is not a good way to interpret the U.S. Constitution." [56] Since then, the politically correct movement has preached that the "separation of church and state" means that America should erase all references to God from this nation. Such nonsense was clearly never the Founders' position, but it has become the position of millions of Americans today. In 1952, U. S. Supreme Court Justice William O. Douglas wrote:

> We are a religious people whose institutions presuppose a Supreme Being. We guarantee the freedom to worship as one chooses. We make room for as wide a variety of beliefs and creeds as the spiritual needs of man deem necessary. We sponsor an attitude on the part of government that shows no partiality to any one group, and that lets each flourish

according to the zeal of its adherents and the appeal of its dogma . . .

To hold that government may not encourage religious instruction would be to find in the Constitution a requirement that the government show a callous indifference to religious groups. <u>That would be preferring those who believe in no religion over those who do believe</u> . . . We find no constitutional requirement which makes it necessary for government to be hostile to religion and to throw its weight against efforts to widen the effective scope of religious influence (emphasis added).[57]

Thank you Justice Douglass! He was right, but his words are hardly ever heard anymore. Since the 1950's, there has been an intentional effort to remove Christianity and religion from the realm of law and government; preferring those who have no religious beliefs, over those who do, in the public square.

A quick history lesson on religion and the U.S. Supreme Court

From 1789 onward, the Bill of Rights applied only to the federal government. Then, in the 1925 case of *Gitlow vs. New York*, the U.S. Supreme Court ruled that the Fourteenth Amendment had made the free-speech and free-press guarantees of the First Amendment operative within the several states. Fifteen years later, in the 1940 decision *Cantwell vs. Connecticut*, the doctrine established in *Gitlow* was extended to apply to the religious freedom clause of the First Amendment to the states.

Empowered by these legal precedents, the first strike came in 1947, with *Everson v. Board of Education*, in which the U.S. Supreme Court ruled that states could not establish a religion, just as the federal government had not been able to establish a religion in the first amendment. The state of New Jersey had been paying for the transportation of students to Catholic schools, and a resident of the

Ewing Township sued that this practice violated the establishment clause of the First Amendment. Although the suit was lost by the plaintiff, Supreme Court Justice Hugo Black made a statement that opened the door to using "separation of church and state" phraseology in constitutional law.

> Neither a state nor the Federal Government can, openly or secretly, participate in the affairs of any religious organizations or groups and vice versa. In the words of Jefferson, the clause against establishment of religion by law was intended to erect "a wall of separation between Church and State."[58]

Then, in the 1962 decision, *Engel v. Vitale*, the Court ruled that the state of New York could not have a morning prayer in schools. The prayer in question was: "Almighty God, we acknowledge our dependence upon Thee, and we beg Thy blessings upon us, our parents, our teachers and our country. Amen." *What an evil thing for school children to repeat every day!* Participation in the prayer had always been voluntary, but the Court said that the prayer was unconstitutional (because of the "separation of church and state").

This landmark ruling (*Engel*) stopped public schools from having prayer at the beginning of each school day, a practice that had been in existence since the founding of this country. Once again, Justice Black argued that there should be a separation of church and state. *Engel* became the basis for several subsequent decisions limiting government-directed prayer in public schools.

In *Wallace v. Jaffree* (1985), the Supreme Court ruled Alabama's law permitting one minute for prayer or meditation was unconstitutional. In *Lee v. Weisman* (1992), the court prohibited clergy-led prayer at high school graduation ceremonies. *Lee v. Weisman*, in turn, was a basis for *Santa Fe ISD v. Doe* (2000), in which the Court extended the ban to school sanctioning of *student*-led prayer at high school football games.

In addition to forbidding prayer in public schools, other court cases sought to keep the Bible out of the school's curricula. In 1963, *Abington School District v. Schempp* found that the policy of beginning the public school day by reading Bible verses was unconstitutional as were the recitations of The Lord's Prayer. *Murray v. Curlett*, a Maryland case involving the son of Madelyn Murray O'Hair, founder of the group American Atheists, was consolidated with Schempp's claim on appeal to the Supreme Court.

In the 1980 decision, *Stone v. Graham*, the Supreme Court found that since there was a constitutional separation of church and state, it would be wrong for public school students to even look, <u>even look voluntarily,</u> at a religious document such as a posting of the Ten Commandments. The Court explained:

> If the posted copies of the Ten Commandments are to have any effect at all, it will be to induce the school children to read, meditate upon, perhaps to venerate and obey the Commandments ... [T]his ... is not a permissible ... objective.

There have been many other rulings since then, but one of the most egregious came down from federal court Judge Samuel Kent in 2000. A high school student, at a Sante Fe public school, was elected by the popular majority of her class to be the "student council chaplain." As such, she regularly gave prayers at the high school football games, in much the same way that thousands of chaplains and ministers have prayed for centuries at the opening of Congress and other governmental gatherings at the state and local level. A few people in the school were offended, so a lawsuit was brought against the school board. In the end, the student was informed that she could no longer pray at these events in the name of Jesus.

Listen to the actual words of Judge Samuel Kent: "The Court will allow that prayer to be a typical non-denominational prayer . . . The prayer must not refer to . . . Jesus . . . or anyone else. . . Anybody who violates these orders, no kidding, is going to wish that he or she had died as a child when this Court gets through with it."[59]

The Results of the Separation

As a result of the absence of Christian values in the government due to the separation of church and state doctrine, we now have the legalized butchering of children in the womb, same-sex marriage and adoption, tax-supported gambling through the state lottery, no-fault divorce laws that leave millions of innocent children in poor single-parent homes, television programs that parade sodomy and pornography through Americans' living rooms every night in the name of "free speech," and a pervasive fear, on the part of pastors, to preach on moral and cultural topics from God's word.

I minister in the state of Tennessee, so let me share with you some state-level results of the abstinence of the church. Even though two-thirds of Tennessee voters in the 2008 Presidential elections identified themselves as evangelical Christians, our state government has been attacking the Christian faith and family for decades.

I mentioned earlier that in 2000, the Tennessee Supreme Court "found" a fundamental right to abortion in the state's constitution? Of course, there are no words of any kind guaranteeing a right to abortion in the state constitution. That was just a matter of philosophical preference on the part of four out of five justices. As a result, all the laws that the legislature had passed (informed consent, 48 hour waiting period, etc.) were struck down. Each year about 14,000 babies lose their lives before they are born in Tennessee. On a per capita basis, Tennessee kills 10,000 babies a year more than Kentucky, simply because Kentucky has passed legislation to control the procedure.

Tennessee is one of only 16 states whose supreme court has "found" a fundamental right to abortion in their state constitution, and we have the only state supreme court that has struck down informed consent laws related to abortion. By applying the judicial review standard known as "strict scrutiny" to the court's ruling, Tennessee has the most liberal constitutional protection of abortion in all fifty states, and our Attorney General has stated that if the people of Tennessee wanted to outlaw the gruesome practice of child slaughter, known as partial-birth abortion, such a ban would be "constitutionally suspect." Even if the U.S. Supreme Court were to ever reverse *Roe v. Wade*, it would do nothing stop the slaughter of the unborn and newly born in this state.

These kinds of battles are raging all over the nation. Focus on the Family has encouraged state-level organizations in 36 states to stand for the family, traditional morality and religious liberty in the state government. They are generally called "family policy councils," and you can learn more about these at the web site: www.citizenlink.com by clicking on "Family Policy Councils" at the top of the web page. You can then search for the one in your state and go to their web site. I strongly encourage all who read this book to find your state FPC and join up ... and donate!

Some Good News!

It wasn't always this bad in America, and it is possible for us to return to our moral foundations. Specifically, on the issue of "separation of church and state," a huge victory took place in 2005 that set organizations trying to erase religion from the nation back on their heels.

In a ruling handed down on December 20, 2005, affirming as constitutional a Ten Commandments display in Mercer County, Kentucky, the U.S. Court of Appeals for the 6th Circuit declared, "The First Amendment does not demand a wall of separation between church and state." The court also criticized the ACLU's repeated reference to the construct, calling it "tiresome" and "extra-constitutional."[60] "For years, the Alliance Defense Fund has argued against claims by the ACLU and its allies that their interpretation of the Establishment Clause is a correct interpretation. The good news for Americans is that today's ruling says the ACLU's interpretation is outside the Constitution. This is a dramatic rollback of the far-left's misguided legal agenda," said ADF Senior Counsel Gary McCaleb. Praise God that somebody can see the plain truth!

Of course, the TV news and newspapers said nothing about this decision, and most Christians have never heard of it because pastors don't usually talk about political things in the pulpit, but it is now part of the legal precedent for constitutional law. A misunderstanding of American history is partially to blame for the success of the ACLU's long tirade against religious freedom. I suppose that if you say something untrue loud enough and long enough, people will eventually begin to believe it. That is exactly what has happened in the U.S. regarding the "separation of church and state." Groups like American Civil Liberties Union, American for Separation of Church and State, Freedom from Religion Foundation, People for the American Way, and others have been reciting their untrue, unconstitutional mantra for so long and so loudly, that many, if not most, American Christians have believed the lie.

The truth is that we were founded as a Christian nation. History proves this, and it is important for churches today to make sure that true history is being passed down to the next generation. If this generation of Christians does not get involved, the next generation may have to pay a high price. Christian Americans live in peaceful times, so far, but one day the ambivalence of the church in the public square may come back to bite us. As Winston Churchill was trying to rally the free world to join the cause opposing the Third Reich, he warned:

> If you will not fight for the right when you can easily win without bloodshed; if you will not fight when your victory will be sure and not too costly; you may come to the moment when you will have to fight with all the odds against you and only a small chance of survival. There may even be a worse case: you may have to fight when there is no hope of victory, because it is better to perish than to live as slaves.

Chapter Three

A Biblical Defense

"Of the many influences that have shaped the United States of America into a distinctive nation and people, none may be said to be more fundamental and enduring than the Bible."[61]

PRESIDENT RONALD REAGAN

As a pastor who is involved in a public policy advocacy organization, I walk the awkward line between religion and politics that most Christians do not care for. I speak to pastors and church leaders on a regular basis about informing their congregations on ways to be involved in the public square, how to start Ethics and Public Affairs Ministries, how to run voter registration drives, how to contact their legislators, etc. Most pastors will preach on cultural and moral issues from time to time, but few have equipped their church members to become engaged in any real, meaningful way. As I've mentioned, I think this comes from a widespread misunderstanding that there should be a separation of church and state. This is such tragedy because throughout human history, God has called upon his children, and especially his chosen prophets, priests and preachers, to speak God's word to rulers.

As you read through the Bible, you cannot help but notice how many times God commands the "called-out ones" (Moses, the prophets, Jesus' followers, etc.) to lobby kings and other rulers of Israel and foreign nations for political outcomes. Elijah was sent by God to confront King Ahab and his wicked Queen Jezebel about their evil treatment of God's children. The prophet Samuel was sent by God to counsel and warn King Saul of his sinful ways. The prophet Nathan brought the warnings of God to King David, Isaiah was sent to King Manasseh, Jeremiah was sent to King Josiah, Daniel and his friends were thrown into the lion's den for their "civil disobedience" to the King Nebuchadnezzar, John the Baptist was beheaded by King Herod for preaching against his immorality, Jesus lectured the Roman Governor, the Jewish Priests, Scribes, Sadducees and Pharisees, Peter displayed civil disobedience, Paul argued his case before the Roman government, and on and on. When God's people are involved in the political arena, the salt and light is applied for the good of the people. The following are a few examples.

Church and State

Biblical Heroes who Brought Faith into the Public Square

As I am making my case that Christians should be salt and light in the public square, I want the reader to understand that this is nothing new. I'm not advocating for some strange, new, cutting-edge ministry in the church. For millennia, God's children have been engaged in politics – often as a response to God's direct commandment. Speaking out against sinful public policies and supporting godly political leaders is something that God's people have been doing for thousands of years. I don't have space to share all the examples from the Bible, but I'll highlight a few of the people who really spoke out as great voices of faith and reason in the public square.

The Old Testament

Joseph

As a case in point, think with me for a moment about the Old Testament son of the Patriarch, Israel, named Joseph. His story is recounted in the later chapters of Genesis. As you may recall, Joseph was a man who loved God and had impeccable character and integrity; nevertheless, Joseph earned a degree from U.H.K. (the University of Hard Knocks). In spite of the harsh circumstances that Joseph went through (i.e. being sold by his brothers into slavery, being falsely accused by an immoral woman, being wrongly imprisoned), God chose to use Joseph to be salt and light in the governmental process. In fact, Genesis 41 records how the Egyptian Pharaoh (the King of Egypt) said:

> Can we find anyone like this man, one in whom is the spirit of God? ... You shall be in charge of my palace, and all my people are to submit to your orders. Only with respect to the throne will I be greater than you." So Pharaoh said to Joseph, "I

hereby put you in charge of the whole land of Egypt" (vs. 37-41).

Joseph was clearly a man of deep religious faith, and God used Joseph's wisdom and political involvement to save His people from a seven-year famine (see Ch. 47). Evidently, when Joseph died there was no one to take his place as a godly influence before the Pharaoh. A frightening thing took place as a result. Exodus 1:6-8 says: "Now Joseph and all his brothers and all that generation died . . . Then a new king, who did not know about Joseph, came to power in Egypt." Guess what happened next? When Pharaoh did not have a "Joseph" in his court, he decided that God's people should become slaves! When the church abandons the state, the godless state will always seek to destroy the church.

It is important to take note of Joseph's preparation for this assignment. Joseph was not a lawyer or a politician. Joseph did not come from a wealthy family or an Ivy League school. For most of Joseph's life, he was a slave or a prisoner. Joseph did not come to politics in order to seize power, to elevate his party to dominance or to conquer his enemies; he came into politics as a servant of Pharaoh, a steward of someone else's power and authority. Just as Romans 13 explains, rulers are stewards of God's authority and must use that authority for the common good just like Joseph did.

Moses

Unfortunately, after Joseph died, the new Pharaoh of Exodus 1 had no man of God in his court, so he saw fit to enslave the children of Israel. He also sought to destroy the Hebrew race through the forced abortion of all the Hebrew male children. Almost four hundred years later, God called another man to be salt and light in the court of the Pharaoh named Moses. Space does not allow for a proper treatment here of the life and work of Moses, but it is important to note a few things about this man of God.

Though he was reared in the lap of royalty, Moses was a shepherd before being called of God to be a political lobbyist. Moses, much like his future descendant David, was a humble shepherd, tending the flocks of his father-in-law, Jethro, when God called him to go to Egypt and lobby for the release of the Hebrew slaves. It is interesting to note how many shepherds were called of God, in the Bible, to lobby kings and rulers on behalf of righteousness and justice. Jesus referred to himself as a shepherd, and ministers of the Gospel today are often called shepherds (the Greek, *poimen*, is rendered shepherd and pastor in the English versions of the Bible), but that is a topic for another discussion.

You might ask, "How can you say that Moses was a lobbyist?" Clearly, Moses was lobbying for a political outcome with Pharaoh, much like political lobbyists do today. A lobbyist is simply someone who advocates for a political outcome by giving politicians information on a bill and the likely benefits or consequences for the politician's constituents. Lobbyists get a bad rap in the media these days, but they actually serve a very wholesome and helpful function in our republican form of democracy. Legislators must vote on hundreds of bills, covering hundreds of issues, and they cannot possibly read and research all the bills for themselves, even with a research staff. Trustworthy lobbyists know all the ins and outs of the issues for which they lobby, and they provide an invaluable service to the legislators when those issues are discussed.

Did you realize that in most states, there are lobbyists for the ACLU, the strip clubs, the liquor industry, the gambling industry, the porn industry, etc? Have you ever wondered if there are any lobbyists representing you, the Christian? The secular lobbyists are highly paid, powerful men and women who have enormous influence on which laws get passed. Who is influencing the legislators on behalf of the family, traditional morality, religious liberty? These are freedoms that most citizens take for granted – until they are lost. As I said in the previous chapter, many states now have a family policy council through the gracious ministry of Focus on the Family. Unfortunately, many states have only one lobbyist representing Christian values – many have no one at all. Visit www.citizenlink.com to learn more about the work being done in your state and do all you can to support them.

Moses lobbied Pharaoh to release the Israelites, and God empowered him with miraculous signs, so Pharaoh finally gave in and released them. If you know the story, Pharaoh changed his mind, as politicians often do, but God supernaturally intervened and set the Israelites free at the Red Sea. For the rest of his life, this shepherd - turned lobbyist - turned emancipator, governed the nation of Israel and codified the "laws of nature and of nature's God." The laws that God gave to Moses, recorded in Exodus, are the foundation of the legal structure in America and most civilized nations. Think of how things might have been if Moses had said to God, at the burning bush, "I'm sorry God, but you can't legislate morality and there's supposed to be a separation of church and state, you know."

Throughout most of world history, kings have had the power to execute anyone found guilty of murder if they felt disposed to do so and there was a witness to the murder. It was Moses' law, from Deuteronomy 19:15, that required the testimony of more than one witness before execution for murder. Jesus commended this judicial principle in Matthew 18:15-17 and instructed his followers to have two or more witnesses present when resolving an interpersonal matter. Since the 14th century, this "due process of law" principle has been enshrined in the criminal jurisprudence of Great Britain, America and other western nations. Moses was a godly man who was the salt of the earth and the light of the world in the public square and the world is a better place for it!

Deborah

Another example of a religious person getting involved in the government in the Old Testament is Deborah. As you may recall from the book of Judges (chapters four and five), Deborah was called by God as the fourth Judge of Israel during the time before the installation of the kings of Israel. Deborah was a humble, devoted wife and mother. She was a dedicated servant of God, and she was used by God to lead the nation to victory in battle and to political peace and prosperity.

Judges 4:1 repeats a phrase that is common in the history of ancient Israel: "After Ehud died (the third Judge),[62] the Israelites once again did evil in the eyes of the Lord." The natural bent of mankind is toward sin, and without Christian or at least morally strong rulers, society will "slouch toward Gomorrah." Judge Robert Bork, a Reagan Supreme Court nominee (1987) who was vilified because of his Christian worldview, wrote an alarming book entitled, Slouching Towards Gomorrah.[63] In it, he warned that America simply must get back to the basics of Christianity if we are to survive as a nation. However, before a people can repent, they must become convicted of their sin; they must first see the problem for what it is. Much like the ancient nation of Israel, we have no righteous rulers to keep us from doing wrong.

There's an old illustration about boiling frogs that says if you drop a frog into a pot of boiling water, he will hop right out, but if you put him in cool water, and slowly raise the temperature one degree at a time, you can cook him without him ever knowing it. (I've used this illustration many times over the years in sermons, but I have to confess I've never tried it. I don't care for cooked frog anyway). To describe the frog-boiling principle in a more intelligent way, Bork cited the "Durkheim Constant." This is a theory, offered by the eminent sociologist Emile Durkheim, which says a society will gradually get used to deviancy by lowering its standards.

What was considered scandalous fifty years ago in American culture is now commonplace, and no one bats an eye. Why? It is not because God's standards have changed; it is because our level of tolerance has changed. As a child, I can remember seeing married couples, like Ozzie and Harriet, portrayed on television sleeping in separate twin beds. Had a television producer in the 1950's shown a couple lying in the same bed, there would have been an outrage across America. Today, one can hardly scan the channels on a typical evening and not see dozens of sexual scenes being graphically displayed during the prime time hours in which millions of children are watching. The other day, I heard my nine year old singing *"Viva Viagra"* after hearing the TV commercial so many times during otherwise family-friendly programming. What has happened? We have become calloused to immorality, and we are no longer outraged.

After Israel suffered the consequences of their moral landslide into sin for twenty years, under the political oppression of the Canaanites, they finally cried out to God for His intervention. Deborah, a married woman who was known as a prophetess, was essentially serving as a one-person Supreme Court of Israel at the time. God spoke to Deborah and commanded her to prophecy to Barack, the leader of the Israeli army (no relation to President Barack Obama, by the way). Barak refused to obey the words of God unless Deborah accompanied him in the battle. Even though Deborah warned him that everyone would say that "God handed over the enemy of Israel to a woman" (vs. 9), Barack insisted that she lead the way.

The army of Israel obeyed the instructions of the Lord, given through the prophetess Deborah, and they were successful in throwing off their military oppressors. In fact, it was a humble woman sitting in a tent that actually killed the leading general of Canaan (vs. 21). What would Israel have done without these two strong women of faith and their willingness to serve in the public square? I have met several strong women of faith who have led the way in establishing ethics and public affairs ministries in their churches, often when the male church leadership would not.

Nathan

When the shepherd boy, David, was anointed King of Israel by the prophet, Samuel, David became another shepherd-turned-politician to lead God's people. David was a good king, and "a man after God's own heart," but he had his share of moral problems. As you recall from the story in II Samuel 11 and 12, David fell into sin with Bathsheba, his neighbor's wife. In an effort to cover up his sins, David sent Bathsheba's husband, Uriah, to the front lines of a battle where he was killed by the enemy. I suppose David thought that he had gotten away with his immoral actions until God sent a preacher named Nathan to confront the king. Nathan appeared before the king, by God's command, and exposed the sinfulness of David's crime. Fortunately, David confessed his sins and repented, something we hardly ever see politicians do today, and Nathan's political involvement brought about a good ending to the story.

Church and State

I want to point out, from the David and Bathsheba story, that God cares about the private behavior of national leaders. When President Bill Clinton was carrying on with his young intern, Monica Lewinski, in the Oval Office, many of his supporters claimed that what an elected official does in private should not have anything to do with his public service. If God felt this way, then he would not have sent Nathan to confront David. God cares about what national leaders do in private because their personal character and integrity – or the lack thereof – has a profound impact on the decisions they make for the country. This is why it is so important that Christians serve in public office and that Christians only vote for candidates who have shown a consistent track record of clean, moral living. In the biblical instructions for leaders of the church, I Timothy 3 forbids a man who cannot properly manage his own household from handling the affairs of the church as an overseer or elder. Should this principle not apply to the government as well?

Nehemiah

Nehemiah, a humble Jew in exile serving the king of Persia as cupbearer, became burdened about the political frailty and national security of Jerusalem. He lobbied King Artaxerxes to fund a campaign to rebuild the walls of Jerusalem and led the people as their governor for many years. It was under the governance of Nehemiah that the remnant of Israel returned from exile and re-instituted worship in the temple and obedience to the Mosaic Law. As a servant and steward of someone else' authority, Nehemiah became a politician and instigated a nation-wide revival as well as many political reforms that benefitted God's children for many years. Oh, that God would raise up a President Nehemiah in the United States today.

Jeremiah

When Jeremiah was but a child, the word of the Lord came to him saying:

> "Before I formed you in the womb I knew you, before you were born I set you apart; I appointed you as a prophet to the nations." God told him, "Get yourself ready! Stand up and say to them whatever I command you. Do not be terrified by them,

or I will terrify you before them. Today I have made you a fortified city, an iron pillar and a bronze wall to stand against the whole land – against the kings of Judah, its officials, its priests and the people of the land."

It's a good thing that Jeremiah's response to God was not, "Sorry, God. Don't you know that you can't legislate morality? And this business about confronting kings and officials with the truth violates the 'separation of church and state too.' All that sounds too political for me." Fortunately, Jeremiah obeyed the Lord and went to the king to lobby on behalf of God's word and the truth.

In Jeremiah 22:3, the prophet proclaimed to the kings and government officials of Judah: "This is what the Lord says: Do what is just and right. Rescue from the hand of his oppressor the one who has been robbed. Do no wrong or violence to the alien, the fatherless or the widow and do not shed innocent blood in this place." Unfortunately, the king and officials would not listen to Jeremiah, and they treated him terribly. I'm sure that Jeremiah often wished that he was not involved in bringing salt and light into the public square. I'm sure he would rather have reasoned to himself: "I just need to forget about all of this prophesying to kings, and just preach to my church members about the joys of getting saved and going to heaven," but Jeremiah could not. He said, "But if I say, 'I will not mention him or speak any more in his name,' his word is in my heart like a fire, a fire shut up in my bones. I am weary of holding it in; indeed, I cannot'" Jeremiah 20:9.

The New Testament

I could go on and on mentioning people in the Old Testament who's salt and light made a huge difference in the public square: Esther, who risked her own life in order to lobby King Xerxes for the salvation of the Jews, Daniel and his three friends who demonstrated "civil disobedience" before King Nebuchadnezzar of Babylon, Amos who told God's people I hate your worship because you ignore injustice, etc. Sometimes Christians think, "All that is good and true about Old Testament prophets and such, but what about Jesus and Christians who now live under the New Testament?" Obviously, Jesus never became an earthly king or ran for office. In fact, he said to Pilate that his kingdom was not of this world. Many have tried to look at Jesus' life and teachings as support for the idea of a separation of church and state, but Jesus never contradicted the teaching of the Old Testament. Although Jesus came to establish a spiritual kingdom, he also taught his followers, by word and by example, that injustice and immorality should be opposed through political engagement.

John the Baptist

After speaking to a crowd of ministers recently, a person approached me and said, "Sure, the Old Testament prophets confronted the kings and tried to be involved in government, but where can you show me that people in the New Testament did that?" I replied, "The very first man of God in the New Testament, who some consider to be the last Messianic Prophet, was John the Baptist. John got his head cut off because he confronted King Herod about his personal immorality and the immorality of his administration. Just as Nathan said it was wrong for King David to have Uriah's wife, and John the Baptist said it was wrong for King Herod to have his brother, Philip's, wife, it is incumbent upon Christians today to confront American political leaders on personal indiscretions as well as public injustices.

Zacchaeus

Zacchaeus was a wee little man who worked as a corrupt Roman tax collector. When he met Jesus, in Luke 19, Zacchaeus was forgiven of his sins and born again. After this transformation, did Zacchaeus leave his job in the government and become a pulpit preacher or a missionary to foreign lands? No, he became a missionary within the government. I have a Christian friend who works for the state department as a senior advisor to the Secretary of State, and there are many good Christians who work for the Internal Revenue Service and other government agencies. We need to teach the young people of our churches that they can be just as effective as missionaries in the government as they can on the foreign mission field.

Jesus

Jesus is often thought of as a great pacifist who opposed the use of force in political change. Jesus grew up in a world dominated by the political oppression of Rome, and many of his followers hoped that he would be a military leader who would empower the Jews to revolt and overthrow the Roman government (Acts 1). Nevertheless, Jesus was not concerned with deposing the Roman rule over the Jews. He was concerned with deposing the satanic rule over the hearts of men and women, but Jesus also cared about social and moral inequities. When Jesus encountered political corruption and injustice, he spoke against it and took decisive action. Jesus said: "Do not suppose that I have come to bring peace to the earth. I did not come to bring peace, but a sword," Matthew 10:34. Let me illustrate this with a few examples.

Jesus confronted corruption and injustice in the courts and legislature. The Senate and House of Representatives of Jesus' day were the Teachers of the Law and the Pharisees. These men passed laws, but they also carried out the role of the judiciary by interpreting laws that previous legislators had passed (the oral law called the Mishnah and Talmud). As Jesus encountered their corruption, he frequently had confrontations with them, and Jesus was not afraid to shine the light on their evil practices – even though he knew they would eventually kill him for it.

In Matthew 23, Jesus preached the Sermon of the Seven Woes. In it, he confronted injustice and corruption of the Jewish lawmakers for passing legislation that they did not keep themselves, usurping respect and honor for themselves that belongs to God, neglecting the weightier matters of the law (justice, mercy and faithfulness), etc. Jesus pulled no punches and called these corrupt legislators "hypocrites," "blind guides," "white washed tombs," "snakes," and "a brood of vipers." Is it any wonder that these legislators wanted to have Jesus killed? It would have been much easier for Jesus to spend all his time healing the sick, feeding the hungry, raising the dead, and preaching about heaven. He did all of those things that we might call "mercy ministries," but Jesus was also deeply concerned about correcting wrongs in the political and cultural arena.

Jesus was the first major historical figure to oppose the ancient tradition of viewing women as property. Jesus taught women (which was unheard of in the ancient world), treated them as people having worth and value in the eyes of God, and instructed his followers to do the same. Jesus, by his own example, advocated for the care of widows, orphans and others who typically were viewed as worthless in the Greco-Roman and Jewish worlds.

Jesus confronted corruption and injustice in the executive branch too. Roman tax collectors were the "scum of the earth" in the eyes of Palestinian Jews of the first century. Many of them were Jews who had betrayed their countrymen, for the sake of personal profit, and they were a hated lot in general. When Jesus encountered two different tax collectors, Matthew and Zacchaeus, the critics complained, "Why does this teacher eat with tax collectors and sinners?" Jesus' reply was: "It is not the healthy who need a doctor, but the sick. But go and learn what this means: 'I desire mercy, not sacrifice.' For I have not come to call the righteous, but sinners," Matthew 9:11-12. Later in Matthew 17 and 22, Jesus instructed his followers to pay their taxes and be law-abiding citizens.

At his trial before the Roman Governor, Pontius Pilate, Jesus explained that he had come to "testify to the truth," John 18:37. Why did Jesus need to testify to the truth in his culture? Isaiah answered that question thousands of years ago: "Justice is driven back, and righteousness stands at a distance; truth has stumbled in the streets, honesty cannot enter. Truth is nowhere to be found, and whoever shuns evil becomes a prey. The Lord looked and was displeased that there was no justice," Isaiah 59:14-15. Still today, Christians need to "testify to the truth" in the public square because sometimes "truth is nowhere to be found" in the modern American culture.

Peter

Peter, perhaps the most quick-tempered and outspoken of Jesus' disciples, instructs us to "Submit yourselves for the Lord's sake to every authority instituted among men: whether to the king, as the supreme authority, or to governors, who are sent by him to punish those who do wrong and to commend those who do right," I Peter 2:13-14. Nevertheless, when the state came into conflict with the church, Peter practiced the civil disobedience exemplified centuries earlier by the prophet Daniel. In Acts 4 and 5, Peter and John were arrested by the law enforcement authorities and rebuked for preaching in the name of Jesus. The freedom of religious expression that Americans enjoy was not permitted in the New Testament period. The Sanhedrin commanded them not to speak or teach at all in the name of Jesus. But Peter and John replied, "Judge for yourselves whether it is right in God's sight to obey you rather than God. For we cannot help speaking about what we have seen and heard," Acts 4:18-20.

Just a few years ago, America was embroiled in great civil unrest over the issue of racism. Many Americans lost their freedom and their lives in the battle for the recognition of blacks as full citizens deserving of equal rights under the law. As Christians had to decide whether or not to become engaged in the civil rights movement, many pastors and other church leaders had to experience their own personal repentance over the sin of racism. In the New Testament, the Apostle Peter went through the same internal conflict. As was quite common among the Jews of the first century, Peter had some pretty strong racial animosity toward Gentiles. The Holy Spirit had to break Peter of this, and did so through a vision about pure and impure foods. Peter finally came to realize that "God does not show favoritism but accepts men from every nation who fear him and do what is right," Acts 10:34-35. Peter could not be content to merely believe that racism was wrong; he had to act on this faith and do whatever he could to end racism. As a result of Peter's new attitude on race, he took the Gospel to the Gentiles of Caesarea. Had Peter not led the charge against the racism of the early Jewish Christians, the Gospel might not have ever reached the Gentiles and most of us, who are not Jews, may have never heard of Jesus Christ.

Paul

Saul of Tarsus was a legal scholar and a rising political star before coming to faith in Christ. As the Apostle Paul, he sought not only to bring the lost to faith in Christ, he also sought to instruct the saved on how to live for Christ in a fallen world. Paul taught believers to understand that the magistrate, or rules, is a servant of God. In Romans 13, Paul explained,

> There is no authority except that which God has established. The authorities that exist have been established by God ... For he is God's servant to do you good. But if you do wrong, be afraid, for he does not bear the sword for nothing. He is God's servant, an agent of wrath to bring punishment on the wrongdoer.

Over and over, Paul uses the word that we frequently translate as servant, minister or deacon – *diakonos* - to describe government officials. He also went to great lengths to help government officials hear the gospel and tried to teach them the ways of Christ.

In Acts 13, we read about the first missionary journey of the early church and right off the bat, the first Christian missionaries (Barnabas and Saul) encountered demonic influence over a government official.

This man, known as Bar-Jesus and Elymas, was evidently a Jew who lived in Paphos on the Island of Cyprus in the Mediterranean Sea (west of Jerusalem). He was a Jew and a political advisor to the Roman Proconsul, Sergius Paulus. A Proconsul was an administrator of civil and military activity in a region and reported to the Roman Senate. It is no surprise that this demon-filled false prophet (Elymas) was involved in influencing government; just as many unbelievers today wield strong political influence in American government.

Bar-Jesus was the man's Hebrew name, and Elymas was the Greek translation. He is reported by the author of Acts to be a *magos*

(Greek), translated into English as magician or sorcerer. It is the same word used of the *magi*, or wise men, in the Gospels who came to see Jesus following the star.

Although Elymas tried to keep Saul and Barnabas from witnessing to the Roman official, they recognized this as spiritual warfare and met it head-on. Through the power of the Holy Spirit, the sorcerer was temporarily blinded, and the Proconsul became a Christian and gave praise to God for what he witnessed.

Many times, Christians conclude that God doesn't care about politics and government, but Saul and Barnabas didn't believe that. Just as the demonic sorcerer, Elymas, knew, Saul and Barnabas also knew that if they could win the Proconsul to Christ and make him a disciple of Jesus, many others would follow his lead and it would be a blessing to all the people.

As with Jesus, Paul took a lot of heat from his political enemies, but he stood his ground. When Paul and Silas were wrongly imprisoned after setting a slave girl free from demons, God miraculously opened the prison doors of the Philippian jail. After this, the guards realized they had illegally arrested a Roman citizen and hoped to release him without public notice. Instead of going away quietly, Paul and Silas appealed to the magistrates that their imprisonment was against the law and demanded a proper, legal acquittal. Paul understood that Christians needed to be salt and light in the realm of law and government.

Paul took on the corrupt business community in Ephesus, especially the lucrative business of making and selling idols to the goddess Artemis. Paul's preaching in the public square about Christ put a serious dent in the profits of the various craftsmen who made these false gods and goddesses. The prominent silversmith, Demetrius, mounted a public relations campaign against Paul that erupted into a riot in the city theater. Fortunately, Paul was spared any physical violence in this verbal altercation, but he made his point clear. Paul was not the kind of Christian to sit idly by when government or the business community promoted immorality.

Church and State

As Paul drew near the end of his years on earth, he sought to pass on his faith and ministry to the young preacher, Timothy. In I Timothy 2:1-2, Paul instructed: "I urge, then, first of all, that requests, prayers, intercession and thanksgiving be made for everyone – for kings and all those in authority, that we may live peaceful and quiet lives in all godliness and holiness." Paul warned Timothy of the price he would have to pay for being salt and light in the culture. "In fact, everyone who wants to live a godly life in Christ Jesus will be persecuted," he said in II Timothy 3:12. There is always a cost for speaking out against corruption and injustice, but faithfulness to the Lord Jesus Christ requires us to speak anyway.

Over and over, throughout the Scriptures, and throughout the history of the church, God has used men and women to be the salt of the earth and the light of the world in the political process. If Christians today shrink back from following these great precedents, and surrender the political process to the god of this world, we will all suffer the consequences of that decision for generations to come.

Historical Christians Who Impacted the Public Square

Thank God that the impact of Christianity did not end with the first believers in Jerusalem. As the book of Acts demonstrates, God sent his burgeoning church throughout the known world to spread the Gospel and redeem fallen humanity. If you take the time to read about the history of the early church, you'll discover that our ancestors in the Christian faith paid a terrible price to evangelize and reform the world around them. During the first three hundred years, the Roman Emperors severely persecuted those whom they called "atheists," because these Christians did not believe in the Greco-Roman pantheon of gods and goddesses. The religious liberty that we so freely enjoy in America was non-existent in the early church era as it still is absent today in many parts of the world. Had it not been for the reformative work of those early believers, our republican form of democracy would not provide the freedoms of religion and conscience that our Constitution gives us today.

The Greco-Roman world before the introduction of Christianity was a showcase of immorality and debauchery. Without the influence of Christ and the Holy Spirit, the natural man creates a society that is a "dog-eat-dog" world. The Greeks and Romans had no political jurisprudence of morals, courtesy, respect for human life, private property, the equality of women with men, etc. All of these values came from the influence of Christians and at what a terrible price!

King Herod, who served the Roman Emperor Nero (54 to 68 A.D.), executed James, the half brother of Jesus, and an immense multitude of Christians during his reign, including the Apostles Paul and Peter.[64] According to the Christian historian Eusebius of the 4th century, "Sometimes ten or more, sometimes over twenty were put to death, at other times at least thirty, and at yet others not far short of sixty; and there were occasions when on a single day a hundred men as well as women and little children were killed."[65] There was a lull in the persecution of Christians during the reigns of Emperors Galba through Titus (68-81), and the church flourished during these years. Surprisingly, however, the church grew more rapidly during the times of intense persecution (under Emperors Domitian through Constantine) than in friendlier times. The 2nd century church father, Tertullian, criticized the Roman government saying: "Your cruelty [against us] does not profit you, however exquisite. Instead, it tempts people to our sect. As often as you mow us down, the more we grow in number. The blood of the Christians is the seed [of the church]."[66]

When Constantine came to power over the Roman Empire, he issued the Edict of Toleration (A.D. 313) that legally put an end to the government persecution of the Christians. As believers in Christ witnessed to their faith in Jesus, through martyrdom, Constantine took notice. Just as the Egyptian Pharaoh remarked of Joseph, the Patriarch, "Can we find anyone like this man, one in whom is the spirit of God?,"[67] Constantine and his royal court of advisors had seen the powerful work of the Holy Spirit that was evident through the early Christians and their faithfulness to the Gospel, even in death. Even

Church and State

Constantine's mother, Helena, had become a Christian. But don't be mistaken: it was not just the preaching of the early Christians that made Constantine sit up and take notice, it was their moral purity and ministry to the needs of the poor and downtrodden that showed him the Way, the Truth and the Life.

Salt and Light in the Early Church Era

Women, children and slaves were mere property in the ancient world before the impact of Christianity, but the early Christians taught the Greco-Roman world that all people have worth and value in the eyes of God. It was the Christians who fought for the establishment of child protective laws, the abolition of abortion, slavery, infanticide, the gladiatorial games and pushed for women's equality under the law in the first centuries of modern history. It is ironic to me that the modern women's liberation movement is so anti-Christian, when the rights that women have to vote, own property (rather than <u>be</u> property), receive an education, hold a job, etc. all came from Christians who brought the values and morality of the Bible into the public square.

In the first few hundred years, A.D., infant girls were largely viewed as worthless property. Historians record that a baby boy was valued, in the male-dominated society, but little girls were often "exposed." Exposure meant that little girls were either thrown away in the refuse heaps to be eaten by wild animals, sold to witches and pagan priests for ritual execution, or sold as slaves. In an ancient letter that has been preserved from history, a Roman businessman wrote to his wife about her pregnancy while he was away:

> Hilarion to Alis his wife: Heartiest greetings . . . Know that we are still even now in Alexandria. Do not worry if when all others return I remain in Alexandria. I beg and beseech of you to take care of the little child, and, as soon as we receive wages, I will send them to you. <u>If – good luck to you! You have a child, if it is a boy let it live; if it is a girl, throw it out.</u> You told

Aphrodisias to tell me: "Do not forget me." How can I forget you? I beg you therefore not to worry (emphasis added). [68]

The sanctity of human life was a Judeo-Christian value that was strange and foreign to the world before Christianity. Often deformed children, and simply unwanted children, were killed or sold as merely a piece of meat. Plutarch (circa A.D. 46-120) speaks of the Carthaginians who, "offered up their own children [in religious ceremonies], and those who had no children would buy little ones from poor people and cut their throats as if they were so many lambs or young birds; meanwhile the mother stood by without a tear or moan."[69] Even the famous philosopher and mentor to Emperors, Seneca, wrote, "We drown children who at birth are weakly and abnormal."[70]

Rescuing and adopting infants that had been abandoned or exposed, Christians engaged the wicked Roman culture with the light of the Gospel and worked to end these practices. Sociologist, Alvin Schmidt, writes, "The Christian opposition to infanticide was not only prompted by their seeking to honor one of God's commandments, 'You shall not kill,' but also by their remembering St. Paul's words, written to them in Rome shortly before Nero had him executed: 'Do not conform any longer to the pattern of this world, but be transformed by the renewing of your mind,'" Romans 12:2.

Just as groups like Focus on the Family, the Right to Life, the Ethics and Religious Liberty Commission and others do today, early Christians published written condemnations of infanticide and abortion.[71] Finally, the Christian emperor, Valentinian – under strong influence by Bishop Basil of Caesarea in Cappadocia, formally outlawed infanticide in A.D. 374.[72]

In A.D. 390, residents of Thessalonica staged a riot against what they perceived to be injustice. Emperor Theodosius the Great squashed the rebellion by having some seven thousands citizens slaughtered, many of whom were innocent Christians. Bishop Ambrose, who was pastor of the church in Milan where the Emperor lived, went to the ruler and lobbied for him to stop the slaughter.

Church and State

Theodosius refused, so Bishop Ambrose ex-communicated him from the church. Eventually, Theodosius stopped the atrocities and repented of his over-reaction.[73]

Christian Views of Sexuality in the Early Church Era

As there was little respect for human life in the pre-Christian world, there was also little respect for God-given sexual mores. In Greco-Roman society, men were legally able to have multiple wives and mistresses. While prostitution was legal for men, married women could be executed for engaging in adultery. In fact, many Roman wives would register as prostitutes with the authorities so that they could not be convicted of adultery. Bestiality, homosexuality, pornography, child molestation, public orgies, etc. were very common in the Greco-Roman culture.[74]

As there is such a push in modern times for the legal recognition of homosexuality in America, it is important for us to realize that no civilization, throughout human history, has survived after homosexuality has become legal.[75] The debauchery of homosexual behavior is a slippery slope. When adult sodomy is legalized or, or even approved of, by society, it is not long before pederasty (or pedophilia, "sexual love of children") becomes legalized as well. Many of the Roman emperors had young boys that they sexually molested as part of their harems, and ancient drawings depict men molesting boys as a common practice. Had Christians not stood against this practice centuries ago, we might not have the laws against pedophiles that we have today.

I fear that we are on a slippery slope in this country today when it comes to the growing homosexual movement. At one time, in America, there were laws against sodomy in all 50 states. Worldwide, and in the U.S., these laws are being ruled "unconstitutional" by courts.

Consider the following regress: In 1994, the British Parliament lowered the age at which it was legal to engage in homosexual acts with boys to age eighteen. Then in 1998, the Parliament again lowered the age limit to sixteen.[76] In Denmark, the age for consensual homosexual sex has been lowered to fourteen. The North American Man/Boy Love Association (NAMBLA), with over one million members in the U.S., seeks to remove all legal restrictions in regard to sex between adult males and boys. In 2000, the television program, *South Park* (on the Comedy Central cable channel) portrayed a child named Eric who unknowingly came in contact with the pedophile group NAMBLA. One of the members blasphemously said, "Thank you Jesus," for sending this boy into their midst to have sex with them.[77] Now, Americans have elected a President (Barack Obama) who has declared, by executive order, June 2009 as Gay, Lesbian, Bi-sexual, Transgendered Month, saying "I want you to know, you [the GLBT community] have the White Houses' support. I will not only be your friend, I will continue to be an ally and a champion and a president who fights with you and for you."[78] What could be next?

Unlike the many passive Christian leaders of today, who refrain from condemning this behavior out of fear of offending or fear of being perceived as judgmental or unloving, the early church spoke out courageously against these sexual immoralities. St. Augustine, of the 5th century, said that the Romans despised Christians for opposing the sexual lasciviousness of their culture.[79] Tertullian wrote that the Romans despised the name "Christian," because of their moral standards.[80] For these offenses to the common practices of reprobation, Christians were sent to the Coliseum where thousands of onlookers cheered as wild animals ripped their bodies to shreds.

More Recent Reforms by Christians throughout the World

In the nation of China, a practice of binding a little girl's feet with bandages, called "foot binding," was practiced for centuries. In the process, a child of four or five years of age would have her foot squeezed at the arch and then bound so tightly that she could not stretch it out. Over time, the foot would grow deformed and gangrenous: often having to be amputated. One Chinese missionary said, "the flesh often became putrescent during the binding and portions sloughed off from the sole; sometimes one or more toes dropped off."[81]

Why in the world was this custom practiced? Evidently, it was to make the girls more sexually arousing to the men. By forcing the big toe down, similar to a woman walking in high heels, the girls would walk more seductively. When Christian missionaries would try to save the girls from this torture, their mothers would re-bind the feet after the church people were out of sight. In fact, the Chinese government frequently condemned the Christians for interfering in this age-old ritual. Finally, in 1912, Christians finally persuaded the government to outlaw the practice.[82]

For hundreds of years, India's practice of *Suttee* (or *Sati*), the burning alive of widows, was an integral part of the Hindu-saturated culture. When a woman's husband died, she was expected to honor him by throwing herself onto his body as both were cremated. If she did not voluntarily commit suicide in this manner, the authorities would physically force her onto the pyre. Because of the Indian practice of adult men marrying child-brides, many children and teenage girls were killed through this practice when their elderly husbands died. Sometimes, they would be burned alive, even while pregnant.[83] As shocking as this practice seems to us today, it was not just isolated to India. History shows that widows were burned alive in pre-Christian Scandinavia, China, the Finns, and in New Zealand. The practice was even recorded among the early Native Americans before the impact of Christopher Columbus and the Christian missionaries.[84]

Of course, Christianity has a much higher view of widows. Based on Jesus' teaching to care for and protect widows (Luke 7, Mark 21, his provision for Mary at the cross, etc.), and the New Testament instructions to look after widows and orphans (James 1:27), the Christians of these societies lobbied hard to have the practice of *Sati* outlawed. Finally, the British authorities in 1829, under the persuasion of Christian Governor-General William Bentinck, outlawed the practice of *Sati*. In 1856, Britain granted Indian widows the right to remarry.[85]

For two millennia, Christians have suffered and died in their efforts to reform and redeem the culture. Much of what we enjoy in modern America: religious liberty, laws against slavery, equality of women, child protective laws, etc., are the results of Christians being salt and light in the public square. Let's fast forward now to the beginnings of American democracy and see how the pilgrims and American settlers built a society of Judeo-Christian principles that became a "shining city on a hill" for the rest of the world.

Chapter Four

Christianity and Early America

"America was born a Christian nation – America was born to exemplify that devotion to the elements of righteousness which are derived from the revelations of Holy Scripture."[86]

PRESIDENT WOODROW WILSON

America began as a nation of Christians who understood that *"Righteousness exalts a nation, but sin is a disgrace to any people."* Nevertheless, America has fallen from her original height in many ways. In the biblical book of the Revelation, Jesus Christ had a message for the church in the city of Ephesus that is pertinent to America today. Consider these words of Christ in Revelation 2:4-5a, *Yet I hold this against you: You have forsaken your first love. Remember the height from which you have fallen! Repent and do the things you did at first ...* Here we see a formula for national revival:

- First, we must realize that we, as a nation, have forsaken Christ, our first love.
- Second, we must remember the height from which we fallen.
- Third, we must repent and do the things that we did at first, the things that made America great.

It is a difficult statement to trace, but the following saying is widely attributed to Alexis de Tocqueville who wrote <u>Democracy in America</u>. He was a French traveler who came to see American democracy first hand during the 18th century. Throughout his travels, Tocqueville found that American religion and government were inseparably mixed like two ropes wound together to form a cord that is stronger than either rope could be alone. Tocqueville is said to have made a wise observation: "America is great because she is good, and if America ever ceases to be good, she will cease to be great." Let me take a moment to remind the reader of the height from which America has fallen.

Influential European Christians who shaped the Freedoms of American Government

In the 15th through 18th centuries, the early formative years of American political thought, several European Christians were widely read by educated Americans, and their ideas were largely responsible for shaping American order. Stephen Langton, Archbishop of Canterbury (essentially the head bishop of the Church in England) was heavily influential in the writing of the Magna Carta. Martin Luther and John Calvin, the powerhouses behind the Protestant Reformation, also were very influential in governmental reforms that reflected biblical principles. John Locke, Baron de Montesquieu, David Hume, and Sir William Blackstone, from France, Scotland, and England, lived and wrote during the days of the atheistic French Enlightenment, but their ideas were much more practical and biblical than that of most of the Enlightenment philosophers. A few cosmopolitan Americans who traveled the world, like Benjamin Franklin, were affected by the Enlightenment doctrines, such as the unbiblical religion of Deism and the exaltation of human reason, but most of the founders of American government held to more traditional Christian views.[87]

Stephen Langton and the Magna Carta

The English barons who forced King John to sign the Magna Carta, at Runnymede in 1215, were the first on the European continent to establish several legal rights that would later be codified in the American Declaration of Independence and the U.S. Constitution and Bill of Rights. The Magna Carta granted that:

1. Justice could not be sold or denied to freemen
2. Taxes could not be levied without representation
3. A citizen could not be imprisoned with a trial, and
4. Property could not be taken by the crown without just compensation[88]

These are principles that Americans may take for granted today, but they were novel ideas to the European peoples of the Dark Ages. The Archbishop of Canterbury, Stephen Langton, was instrumental in the writing and birth of the Magna Carta along with several other Christians of influence. Langton called these principles that restricted the powers of the king the "Ambrose Principle," referring to the heroic lobbying of Bishop Ambrose I mentioned above. Langton is also credited with dividing the English Bible into chapters.

Martin Luther

In the year A.D. 1520, Martin Luther, the instigator of the Protestant Reformation, wrote of two kingdoms or two realms: the church and the state. He believed that the state should not govern the church and the church should not govern the state. Luther was reacting to centuries of the abuse of power that the Roman Catholic Church had acquired throughout the Dark Ages. Luther's two realms did not mean that Christians should abandon the state and keep quiet, he simply meant that the state was to govern temporal, earthly affairs, and the church was to govern spiritual, eternal affairs. Quoting Jesus' admonition to "render unto Caesar that which is Caesar's and unto God that which is God's," he taught that Christians have a responsibility in both realms. Luther advocated that the kings and other rulers should be evangelized and catechized (discipled) if at all possible, but he was an advocate of the state being led by Christian laity rather than the Catholic hierarchy.[89]

Luther strongly believed in religious freedom, and he turned the Roman Catholic Church upside down in defending his belief. For centuries, the church and state had become inseparably mingled, and often times the state had executed heretics and non-believers as bidding for the Catholic Church. The Inquisitions (A.D. 844-1834) were evidence of what happens when the organized Church wields the power of the magistrate and punishes unorthodox beliefs as though they are criminal behaviors. Over Roman Catholic doctrinal controversies such as the actual meaning of Christ's body and blood being present in the bread and cup of Communion (transubstantiation vs. consubstantiation), godly men such as John Hus and Jerome Savonarola were burned alive for their defiance to official Church doctrine. When Luther came along, he challenged this intertwining of church and state powers, saying that it was not the function of the government to "forbid anyone to teach or believe or say what he wants – the Gospel or lies."[90] At great personal risk, Luther told Emperor Charles V, in the Diet of Worms:

Church and State

> Unless I am convicted by Scripture and plain reason – I do not accept the authority of popes and councils, for they have contradicted each other – my conscience is captive to the Word of God. I cannot and will not recant anything, for to go against conscience is neither right nor safe. God help me, Amen.[91]

Luther's defiance to a church-run state did not fall on deaf ears by the American founders. The secular historian, Thomas Bailey, called Martin Luther one of the "indirect founding fathers of the United States."[92]

John Calvin

John Calvin was the primary reformer of the Roman Catholic Church in Geneva, and his immense theological work, The Institutes of the Christian Religion, set out the basic doctrines that much of modern Christianity espouses, i.e. the priesthood of the believer, salvation by grace rather than through religious works, the perseverance of believers, etc. In addition to Calvin's theological work, he was also a political reformer.

Calvin drafted the new ordinances that the government modified and adopted as a constitution for Geneva governing both secular and sacred matters. Calvin also supported development of a municipal school system for all children with the Geneva Academy as the center of instruction for the very best students. In 1559 the academy was begun with Theodore Beza as Rector of what eventually became a full university.

Calvin sought to improve the life of his fellow citizens in many ways. He supported good hospitals, a proper sewage system, protective rails on upper stories to keep children from falling from tall buildings, special care for the poor and infirmed, and the introduction of new industries.

Calvin's Institutes addressed Civil Government (Book IV, Chapter 22) and outlined much of what Americans have come to take for granted as sensible government. Calvin addressed the separate roles of church and state regarding the enforcement of laws, outlined the chief tasks of government, based upon Scripture, defended the place of the magistrate as an ordained delegation of God's authority, etc.

Calvin explained the necessity of the civil government to tax and spend tax moneys for the benefits of the commonwealth. He explained that it is honorable for the magistrate to raise taxes but that these should not be excessive. In fact Calvin's statement on excessive taxation rang true in the war for independence from Great Britain, and it rings true in America today: "The imposts and levies, and other kinds of tributes are nothing but the supports of public necessity; but that to impose them upon the common folk without cause is tyrannical extortion."

John Locke

The Christian physician and political philosopher, John Locke, wrote Two Treatises of Government in 1690. He postulated that the natural law given by God to Moses should be respected in statutory law. To Locke, the tyrannical abuses of the kings clearly violated God's natural law and the rights of mankind. Locke was one of the first to suggest that human rights come, not from government, but from God and through the consent of the governed. Though Locke has been referred to as a Deist, he frequently quoted the Scriptures as proof-texts of his points and wrote of his personal faith in Jesus Christ in The Reasonableness of Christianity (1695).

Baron de Montesquieu

At the Constitutional Convention of 1787, no author was more frequently quoted than Charles Louis de Secondat, Baron de Montesquieu (1689-1755). His major work, The Spirit of Laws,[93] laid out the notion of separation of powers that would play such a crucial role in the three branches of American government.[94] Did you know that the three branches of government actually come from the Bible? Isaiah 33:22 says, "For the Lord is our judge, the Lord is our lawgiver, the Lord is our king; it is He who will save us."

Montesquieu believed in the existence of natural law, which had been taught by Plato, Cicero, Aquinas, Hooker and others for centuries. "Before laws were made, there were relations of possible justice. To say that there is nothing just or unjust but what is commanded or forbidden by positive (or written) laws, is the same as saying that before the describing of a circle all the radii were not equal." In other words, the circle existed long before men called it a circle, and natural law has always existed, even if mankind does not codify it in a law book or constitution.

On such principles, Montesquieu stood against the common practice of human slavery. Even though the written laws of man said that some people were less than human and not worthy of basic human rights, Montesquieu believed that the practice was morally wrong. Were he alive today, I am confident that Montesquieu would have worked to end legalized abortion for the same reasoning. In the same line of reasoning on slavery, we must recognize the fact that abortion is morally wrong by natural law, even if the U.S. Supreme Court says it is not.

Montesquieu also contributed some significant thoughts on the separation of church and state and the power that the state has over the church when the church seeks tax-exemption and other "favors" from the state. Montesquieu wrote:

> A more certain way to attack religion is by favor, by the comforts of life, by the hope of wealth; not by what reminds one of it, but by what makes one forget it; not by what makes one indignant, but by what makes men lukewarm, when other passions act on our souls, and those which religion inspires are silent. In the matter of changing religion, State favors are stronger than penalties.[95]

David Hume

Another influential European political philosopher that had a tremendous impact on the men who shaped American government was the Scot, David Hume. Alexander Hamilton, in The Federalist 85, called Hume "a writer equally solid and judicious." Hume was passionately anti-philosophy, meaning that he rejected exaltation of human reason over biblical revelation. Hume wrote against the "liberals" of his day saying: "Why rake into those corners of nature, which spread a nuisance all around? The obsessions of philosophers with abstract reason, a priori systems, and unprofitable teachings tend toward injury to society." Were Hume alive today, he would probably say the same thing about the unbiblical notions that are taught so widely in American universities (evolution, secular humanism, Freudian psychology, etc.).

Sir William Blackstone

Perhaps the most influential legal writer of the early-American period was Sir William Blackstone (1723-1780). A devout Christian and Oxford professor of law from England, Blackstone published his Commentaries on the Laws of England in 1765. Blackstone's Commentaries became the Bible of American lawyers until the late 1820's. In the late 1700s, Americans increasingly turned to the Commentaries of Blackstone as a model for the legal system of a democratic republic. The natural law of Sir William Blackstone was rooted in the Christian faith, and his book was the legal textbook for practically all American lawyers and judges for decades after the War for Independence. On the existence of natural law, or the law of nature's God, Blackstone wrote:

> This law of nature, being co-equal with mankind and dictated by God himself, is of course superior in obligation to any other. It is binding over all the globe, and all countries, and at all times; no human laws are of any validity if contrary to this; and such of them as are valid derive all their force, and all their authority, mediately or immediately from this original."

This law of nature would become that law to which the American revolutionaries would appeal in their argument to take up arms against the oppressive laws of England's King George III. The same law of nature tells us today that sodomy is a perversion of nature, even if the courts say it is merely another form of marriage. The laws of nature and of nature's God tell us that it is wrong to call pornography "free speech" and spew it into the living rooms of millions of Americans through the television and the internet. The laws of nature and of nature's God gives mankind the ability to discern good from evil when the written laws of men cannot rightly distinguish the two.

William Wilberforce

William Wilberforce was a member of the English Parliament during the late 1700's and early 1800's, and he fought tirelessly for the abolition of the slave trade in England. I highly recommend that you see the movie made about him called "Amazing Grace."[96] In the late 1700's, British traders raided the coast of Africa and captured tens of thousands of men, women and children each year and shipped them across the Atlantic to be sold as slaves. When Wilberforce learned of this, his intuitive sense of justice and righteousness impelled him to do something about it.

Later in life, Wilberforce would write of his decision to use politics to abolish slavery saying:

> So enormous, so dreadful, so irremediable did the trade's wickedness appear that my own mind was completely made up for abolition. Let the consequences be what they would: I from this time determined that I would never rest until I had effected its abolition.

Beginning in 1789, Wilberforce and his companions introduced legislation in the British Parliament to abolish the slave trade, but it was defeated. Year after year, Wilberforce worked against this corrupt industry with little success. I'm sure some of Wilberforce's Christian friends advised him to give up the effort after so many defeats. I wish I could talk with him, because I would be willing to bet Wilberforce heard an earful from clergy who said that "you just can't solve societies' moral problems through politics." But Wilberforce would not quit. He knew that the horrors of slavery would not end because English Christians became more spiritual, prayed more, went to church more, etc.: it would only end when the practice of slavery was illegal and punishable by law. In 1807, Wilberforce and his friends finally won the victory they had sought for so many years: British Parliament abolished slavery.

Lord Shaftesbury

Another champion of salt and light in the public square during the 19th century of England was Anthony Ashley Cooper, Lord Shaftesbury. Shaftesbury served for a number of years in the British Parliament, and his determined commitment to be salt and light was noted by the famous preacher, Charles Spurgeon, saying, "A man so firm in the gospel of Jesus Christ, so intensely active in the cause of God and man, I have never known."[97] In the beginning of the Industrial Revolution, English boys and girls, from poor families or from no families, often ended up working 12-16 hour days in the deplorable conditions of the coal mines and factories. Godly men like Lord Shaftesbury simply could not look upon this injustice and pretend that it did not exist.

Shaftesbury, as well as other better known advocates of child labor laws like William Wilberforce and the novelist, Charles Dickens, took it upon themselves to rid their "Christian" county of the horrid child labor industry. At age 26, Shaftesbury wrote, "I want nothing but usefulness to God and my country."[98] Through tireless efforts, Shaftesbury succeeded in passing the Factory Act of 1833 that limited the number of hours that a child under the age of 13 could work to 48 per week. In the 1840's, Shaftesbury was successful at passing further legislation to protect children from inhumane working conditions. Laws continued to improve thereafter, and eventually all child labor was banned in the English factories, mills and mines. The United States, Germany, France and other countries followed suit and even as recently as 1938, the U.S. enacted the Fair Labor Standards Act.

If you will now take a trip with me on an imaginary ship, we are going to set sail from the western shores of the British Isles and head toward the continent we now know as the United States of America: the land of the free and the home of the brave. Since the days of the first pilgrims who landed on the shores of Plymouth, Christian men and women in America have been fighting for truth, righteousness and the Christian way of life in our great nation.

Church and State

American Founding Fathers who were Salt and Light in the Public Square

The founders of America knew the Bible, and because of their Christian faith, they intuitively knew that taxation without representation was wrong, that the rights of mankind were given by God, not a king or parliament, and that there was a natural law created by God. This is why they claimed, in the Declaration of Independence, "We hold these truths to be self-evident, that all men are created equal, that they are endowed by their Creator with certain unalienable Rights, that among these are Life, Liberty and the pursuit of Happiness."

All of our original governing documents and guiding principles were birthed out of the Christian religion, and most of the formative rallies for independence were held in Christian churches. For example, the role of the Christian church in the struggling Colony at Jamestown, Virginia, is too little known. Historian Mark Noll reminds us:

> As soon as the first settlers arrived in May 1607...they joined the Rev. Robert Hunt... in holding a service of communion. When Lord De La Warr, a new governor arrived in 1610 as the colony teetered on the brink of collapse, his first action was to organize a worship service in order to issue a biblical call for sacrifice and industry. Virginia's earliest legal code made attendance at Sunday services compulsory...

Imagine the outcry if an American governor issued such a proclamation today!

> Consider this remarkable, mostly unknown occurrence: As fresh winds of hope and prosperity began to blow into the struggling colony, the ideal of self-government was taking root in the soil of their souls. The first meeting of an elected legislature in what would become the United States took place on July 30, 1619, *in the Jamestown church!* This was the same

church were Pocahontas professed her faith in Christ, was baptized, took on the Christian name "Lady Rebekah," and married John Rolfe in 1614. The truth is that at numerous, decisive moments in our nation's history, a pastor and the church were there, giving guidance, courage, and correction. This glorious legacy must not die with us. By God's grace, it will not.[99]

During the colonial period, prior to the fight for independence from England, America was almost exclusively a Christian nation. The laws of the land were the laws of the Bible, and sin was preached against in the churches and the schools. The government was charged with punishing sin and keeping society morally pure. In fact, one act of the Massachusetts colony said: "No custom nor prescription shall ever prevail amongst us . . . that can prove to be morally sinful by the Word of God." What would the Massachusetts colonists have thought of the modern state of Massachusetts' legalization of same-sex marriage today and her openly homosexual Senator Barney Frank?

John Quincy Adams, Sixth President of the United States, wrote about God's natural law and its place in practically all governments:

> The law given from Sinai was a civil and municipal as well as a moral and religious code; it contained many statutes ... of universal application-laws essential to the existence of men in society, and most of which have been enacted by every nation which ever professed any code of laws.[100]

At the heart of this matter, the question often arises, "Was America founded as a Christian nation?" The answer to that question is impeccably clear: yes! During my Ph.D. work, I researched this question in great detail, and have found that those men who signed the Declaration, fought the revolutionary war, and framed the U. S. Constitution, better than anyone else, are best fit to provide an answer. What did the founders of this nation think of the interplay between the church and the state? Consider these facts:

Of the 55 colonial delegates to the Constitutional Convention of 1787, 52 (roughly 95%) were members of Christian churches, and the majority of them held degrees from Bible colleges and seminaries. Contrary to the widespread, but false, information about the prevalence of Deism among the framers, only 3 of the delegates considered themselves to be such (merely 5.5%).[101] Even these three Deists would be shocked to discover how modern Americans have tried to twist and contort history to wage war against Christianity in the public square. In fact, the Congress of 1854 stated:

> Had the people, during the Revolution, had a suspicion of any attempt to war against Christianity, that Revolution would have been strangled in its cradle ... In this age, there can be no substitute for Christianity ... That was the religion of the founders of the republic and they expected it to remain the religion of their descendants.[102]

One can ascertain the worldview of the framers of the Constitution by reading their writings. Research in a 1984 article appearing in the *American Political Science Review* detailed a study of over 17,000 written works by the Framers during the era of the late 1700's.[103] One might conclude that the sources quoted by these writers would indicate the books that they were reading. Did you know that of the quotations from other works that the framers cited in their writings, 34% came from the Bible? The two most oft-cited non-biblical writers were Baron Charles Montesquieu and Sir William Blackstone: two European legal writers, as I've previously mentioned, with clearly biblical views of law and government.[104]

If this is not convincing proof that America was founded by Christians, consider the words and actions of the founders themselves:

Thomas Jefferson

The principle author of the Declaration of Independence, Thomas Jefferson was not what people today would call an evangelical Christian, but he was learned in the Scriptures and professed a deep faith in a Supreme Being/Creator. Only later in life, did Jefferson become a member of the sect known as Deism that denied many of the biblical doctrines including the sinfulness (depravity) of man.

Juxtaposed to the influential writing of the other founders, Jefferson mostly kept his uncommon theological views to himself. As President, he wrote to Benjamin Rush saying that he would not publish his <u>The Life and Morals of Jesus</u>, (Jefferson's take on the New Testament) for fear that his views would "countenance the presumption of those who have endeavored to draw them before that tribunal, and to seduce public opinion to erect itself into that inquest over the rights of conscience, which the laws have so justly proscribed." In other words, if it got out that Jefferson differed from the rank and file American Christian on theological issues, he and his party would be in big trouble.

Jefferson coined the term "Natures' God," by which he meant the Supreme Being that created and governs the world, but Jefferson did not view this God to necessarily be Jesus or even the God of the OT. On the other hand, the American people generally held to the God of the Bible, and the spiritual legacy of Jonathan Edwards, the Puritan evangelist, would be considered the foundation of the political philosophy of the Democratic Party under the administration of President Jackson.[105]

Nonetheless, Jefferson was raised in a Christian culture and was well versed in the words of the Bible. Like practically all Americans of his day, biblical themes and doctrines were part of Jefferson's notions of right and wrong. When the Capitol building was completed in 1800, Christian worship services were held each Sunday morning in the Hall of the House. Then-President Jefferson not only attended the Sunday services on a regular basis, but he ordered the Marine Band to play in the services. Jefferson also began church services in the War Department building and the Treasury building allowing Americans a choice of places to worship in Washington D.C. if they wished, and by 1853, the church at the Capitol was the largest congregation in Washington with some 2,000 worshippers in attendance on any given Sunday. Jefferson also urged local governments to make land available for Christian purposes. He provided federal funding for missions work among the Native American tribes and declared that religious schools should receive the patronage of the government.

Church and State

On the Jefferson memorial, in Washington D.C., one finds these words engraved: "God who gave us life, gave us liberty at the same time. Can the liberties of a nation be secure when we have removed their only sure basis, a conviction in the midst of the people that those liberties are the gifts of God?" Does that statement sound like someone who did not believe in the importance of Christian values being preserved through government?

George Washington

When Washington received a copy of the Declaration of Independence from the Continental Congress, he immediately issued orders that "The Colonels or commanding officers of each regiment are directed to procure Chaplains accordingly; persons of good Character and exemplary lives." On July 9, 1776, General Washington ordered, "The blessing and protection of Heaven are at all times necessary but especially so in times of public distress and danger. The general hopes and trusts that every officer and man will endeavor to live and act as becomes a Christian soldier, defending the dearest rights and liberties of his country."[106] After he led the Continental Army to victory in the War of Independence, Washington presided over the Constitutional Convention and was then elected our first president under the Constitution. Throughout his years of public service, Washington daily read his Bible, prayed for guidance, and attended church on Sundays.

At Washington's first inauguration in New York City, the great leader took the oath of office on a Bible opened to Genesis 49 and 50, and uttered the words repeated by every president since, "So help me God." He told his audience at Federal Hall that, "It would be peculiarly improper to omit, in this first official act, my fervent supplications to that Almighty Being who rules over the universe, who presides in the councils of nations." Washington then went, very publicly, to pray at St. Paul's Chapel before he attended inaugural festivities.

Eight years later, in his farewell address, Washington said, "Of all the dispositions and habits which lead to political prosperity, religion and morality are indispensable supports." Washington, as perhaps the leading founding father, demonstrated repeatedly that religion has a legitimate place in the public square. Today's complaints and lawsuits over the Ten Commandments monuments would seem ludicrous to Washington and to all who served with him.

Was George Washington a Christian? His granddaughter, Nelly Custis, lost her father in death as a child. The President and Mrs. Washington adopted young Nelly. For twenty years, she and her mother lived in the Washingtons' home. In her diaries, Nelly wrote of the great General, her grandfather, and spoke of his daily quiet times in prayer and Bible reading. She spoke of his attendance at church. He never missed. In fact, he sat up front in church (she said "His pew was near the pulpit") and stood throughout the giving of the sermon, as was the custom then to honor the preaching of the word of God (what a drastic contrast to the comfortable, seeker-focused worship in many churches of the modern era). Of course only God knows the heart, but if this man was not a Christian, in my mind, there has never been one.[107]

John Adams

Adams was the second president of the United States and was involved in all of the founding activity of the country. Being one of only two Founders to sign the Bill of Rights, Adams was a constitutional expert. He declared that the American experiment in a republican form of democracy would not work if the nation were to ever divorce Christian morality from the government. Adams wrote, "The general principles on which the fathers achieved independence were ... the general principles of Christianity."[108] Christianity was interwoven throughout the building of this great country. Early American historian, Richard Hildreth, wrote, "The Church and State were most intimately blended. The magistrates and general court, aided by the advice of the (church) elders, claimed and exercised a supreme control in spiritual as well as temporal matters; while even in matters purely temporal the elders were consulted on all important questions."[109]

If President John Adams were alive today and addressed our nation, I'm confident that he would sharply rebuke those who are trying so hard to remove Christianity from the political sphere.

Adams wrote:

> [W]e have no government armed with power capable of contending with human passions unbridled by morality and religion . . . Our Constitution was made only for a moral and religious people. It is wholly inadequate to the government of any other.[110]

Patrick Henry

Patrick Henry was a delegate (VA) to the First Continental Congress in 1774 and an influential leader in the Revolutionary War. He was also instrumental in writing the Declaration of Independence. He is most famous for a speech made in 1775 at St. John's Church in Virginia (*a political speech in church*) in which he bellowed, "Is life so dear or peace so sweet as to be purchased at the price of chains and slavery? Forbid it, Almighty God. I know not what course others may take, but as for me, give me liberty or give me death!"[111] This great Christian patriot must have known that one day Americans would doubt the Christian foundation of the nation, for he wrote,

> It cannot be emphasized too strongly or too often that this great nation was founded, not by religionists, but by Christians; not on religions, but on the gospel of Jesus Christ. For this reason peoples of other faiths have been afforded asylum, prosperity, and freedom of worship here.[112]

Patrick Henry also reminded us, "It is when a people forget God that tyrants forge their chains." To Henry and the other framers, America was not designed to be a religious dictatorship with Christianity as the state religion. This would have been no different than what we saw with Saddam Hussein and his government of radical Islam in Iraq. Because the nation's founders were believers in Christ, they knew that religion had to be "from the heart," and not "from the state."

The framers were happy for people of other faiths to live in America and worship as they please. Persons of all faiths are free to exercise their religion in the United States. The First Amendment guarantees that right. But one should not think that America was founded on religious pluralism or atheism: far from it. America was founded on the principles of biblical Christianity. Henry knew that the principles of Christianity were the principles that would make America great. He wrote, "The general diffusion of Christian knowledge hath a natural tendency to correct the morals of men, restrain their vices, and preserve the peace of society."[113]

John Jay

John Jay served as the first Chief Justice of the U.S. Supreme Court, appointed by President George Washington, and was a member of the First and Second Continental Congresses. Jay, along with James Madison and Alexander Hamilton, was an author of the Federalist Papers that outlined in great detail the philosophical underpinnings of our national government. In addition to serving on the U.S. Supreme Court, Jay was also elected as President of the American Bible Society in 1821. In this role, Jay wrote, "The Bible is the best of all books, for it is the word of God and teaches us the way to be happy in this world and in the next. Continue therefore to read it and to regulate your life by its precepts."[114]

In a day and age, when millions of Christian Americans do not vote in our elections, many of whom are not even registered to vote, the words of John Jay are especially convicting: "Providence has given to our people the choice of their rulers, and it is the duty, as well as the privilege and interest of our Christian nation to select and prefer Christians for their rulers."[115] As I write this book, Obama's nominee to the U.S. Supreme Court, Sonya Sotomayor, has just been confirmed by the U.S. Senate. She replaces retired Justice David Souter, and she joins the other liberal justices whose views are antithetical to those espoused by John Jay and the early justices. How we should heed the advice of William Patterson, a signer of the Constitution and a U.S. Supreme Court Justice: "When the righteous rule, the people rejoice; when the wicked rule, the people groan," invoking Proverbs 29:2 to instruct a grand jury.[116]

Church and State

Dr. Benjamin Rush

Dr. Benjamin Rush was a signer of the Declaration of Independence, the Surgeon General of the Continental Army, a Framer of the U.S. Constitution, known as the "Father of American Medicine," Treasurer of the U.S. Mint, and known as the "Father of public schools under the Constitution." He wrote, "The only means of establishing and perpetuating our republican forms of government is the universal education of our youth in the principles of Christianity by means of the Bible."[117] That is a powerful statement, especially in light of the pervasive secularism in today's public school system. In 1777, America faced a shortage of Bibles for children to read in the schools. To solve the problem, the U.S. Congress ordered 20,000 copies of the Bible to be used in public schools throughout the nation.

My wife is a public school teacher, as was my mother, sister and mother-in-law. I've seen the "ins and outs" of public education all of my life, and there is not one doubt in my mind that America is falling apart morally because American children are not taught the truth of God's word, in the schools and in the home. Our school-age children spend 40 or more hours a week being taught and indoctrinated by textbooks from which God and Christian values have been erased. While there are many wonderful Christian teachers in the public system, most feel restricted in teaching the truth of God's word for fear of being fired or sued. Consider another remark by Dr. Rush:

"The great enemy of the salvation of man, in my opinion, never invented a more effective means of limiting Christianity from the world than by persuading mankind that it was improper to read the Bible at schools."[118] How I wish our government understood this concept today.

If Satan wants to attack God by decimating the ranks of the churches, and he does, there is no more potent method than for him to fill the young, impressionable minds of American youth with secular humanism, evolution and moral relativism. It is no different in America today than it was in the days of the prophet Daniel, under the wicked kingdom of Nebuchadnezzar.

In the third year of the reign of Jehoiakim king of Judah, Nebuchadnezzar king of Babylon came to Jerusalem and besieged it . . . Then the king ordered Ashpenaz, chief of his court officials, to bring in some of the Israelites from the royal family and the nobility – young men without any physical defect, handsome, showing aptitude for every kind of learning, well informed, quick to understand, and qualified to serve in the king's palace. <u>He was to teach them the language and literature of the Babylonians</u> (Daniel 1:1-5).

For decades now, churches in America have seen a declining participation by the younger generations, and in many American churches there simply are no youth in attendance. Along with this decline in church attendance among our youth, there has been a sharp increase in immorality among their generation. Noah Webster, a legislator, educator and author of <u>Webster's Dictionary</u>, wrote, "All the ... evils which men suffer from vice, crime, ambition, injustice, oppression, slavery and war, proceed from their despising or neglecting the precepts contained in the Bible."[119] As the American church gets grayer and emptier, we are seeing a generation of young people who have no idea that the Bible speaks truth and freedom to every aspect of their lives. How can we make a change in this culture if American Christians stay out of the public square?

James Madison

James Madison was a Christian who spent over half a century in public service. A principle author of the <u>Federalist Papers</u>, Madison is often called "The Father of the Constitution." Madison was the youngest delegate to the Continental Congress, a signer of the Declaration of Independence, a member of the Constitutional Convention, a Virginia congressman, the fourth President of the U.S. and the main author of the Bill of Rights.[120]

In an eerily prophetic way, Madison must have known that one day Americans might question the constitutionality of the Ten Commandments and other Christian symbols in the public square. He wrote, "We have staked the whole future of American civilization, not upon the power of government, far from it. We have staked the future of all our political institutions upon the capacity of each and all of us to govern ourselves, to control ourselves, to sustain ourselves according to the Ten Commandments of God (emphasis added)."[121]

In the first several hundred years of American occupation of the new world, the Christian faith was interwoven into the fabric of the widespread notion of American liberty. From his studies of early American history, Russell Kirk observed that:

> It was America's moral order, then, that sustained America's social order ... even though the common man of the West seemed interested chiefly in his own material aggrandizement – still he read his Bible, accepted as good the political framework which he inherited from the Atlantic seaboard and from Britain, and took for granted a moral order that was his custom and his habit.[122]

As Tocqueville observed, "For the Americans, the ideas of Christianity and liberty are so completely mingled that it is almost impossible to get them to conceive of one without the other; it is not a question with them of sterile beliefs bequeathed by the past and vegetating rather than living in the depths of the soul."[123]

I could go on and on quoting from the founding fathers of this country, but let me turn now to our two founding documents: the Declaration of Independence and the U.S. Constitution for proof that the founders of this country recognized that it was a Christian society.

Chapter Five

Freedom Rests upon Biblical Principles

"If the spirit of God is not in us and if we will not prepare to give all that we have and all that we are to preserve Christian civilization in our land, we shall go to destruction. We cannot read the history of our rise and development as a nation without reckoning with the place the Bible has occupied in shaping the advances of the Republic."[124]

PRESIDENT FRANKLIN DELANO ROOSEVELT

"Where the Spirit of the Lord is, there is freedom."

II Corinthians 3:17

Church and State

A free church in a free state: what an ideal. Each organization functions independently, without one controlling the other. This was the desire of our nation's founders who were fed up with the control that the Church of England (and formerly the Roman Catholic Church) held over the people of the British Isles. But let's pause to consider what a free church in a free state means.

In order to have a free church, there must be a free state. A government that does not respect the rights of individuals to life, liberty and the pursuit of happiness, which happen to be religious principles, will not respect the rights of conscience and religious expression either. So if the church wants to have religious freedom, there must be a governmental respect for freedom.

The converse of this is also true: a free state requires a free church. If the church is bound to a political control that denies individual religious expression and the rights of conscience, or is driven out of the nation entirely, that oppression will be mirrored in the government, and the government will become cruel and oppressive over all its citizens.

The Scripture quoted at the beginning of this chapter says, "Where the Spirit of the Lord is, there is freedom (or liberty)." If biblical Christianity is present in the culture, freedom will force its way through the halls of government like a flower pushing through a crack in the concrete sidewalk. Conversely, if the Spirit is absent from the realm of government, you can be sure that there will be no freedom.

A government which has not been influenced by authentic Christianity (through citizen engagement, rather than ecclesiastical force) will quickly turn into a godless dictatorship. Look at the history of leaders like Hitler, Mussolini, Stalin, etc. As I mentioned earlier in the book, when the Pharaoh did not have a "Joseph" in his court (Exodus 1:8), he enslaved God's people and destroys their freedom. It is imperative for Christians to understand that it is their presence and influence in the government that allows freedom to flourish in both the state and the church!

The liberty that Americans enjoy comes from "the laws of nature and of nature's God," as the Declaration of Independence put it, and those laws are spelled out in the Bible. In the words of Daniel Lapin, the founders modeled themselves "upon God's ancient people" and "wrote what they considered to be a modern-day interpretation of the basic biblical principles of government."[125]

Declaration of Independence

The Declaration, which motivated Washington's appointment of military chaplains, contains four references to God:

1. God as the Creator and the source of liberty ("all men are endowed by their Creator with unalienable rights")
2. God the law giver ("law of nature and of nature's God")
3. God the ultimate judge ("the Supreme Judge of the World"), and
4. God as the king above all earthly rulers, as the Sovereign ("Divine Providence").

Of course, we know that the Bible teaches us that God is our creator, but did you know that the Bible gave us the three branches of government: executive, judicial and legislative? Isaiah 33:22 teaches *"For the Lord is our judge, the Lord is our lawgiver, the Lord is our king; it is he who will save us."*

Some say that the Declaration is nothing more than a document of ideals and has nothing to do with the law, but the U. S. Supreme Court has repeatedly cited the Declaration of Independence as part of the fundamental law of the United States of America.[126] The United States Code, Annotated includes the Declaration under the heading "Organic Laws of the United States of America" along with the Articles of Confederation, the Constitution, and the Northwest Ordinance. Constitutional law professor, John Eidsmoe, states, "The Constitution is built on the Declaration of Independence, and the Declaration finds practical expression in the Constitution. Neither can be fully understood without the other."[127]

U. S. Constitution

The U. S. Constitution does not quote Scripture nor express religious views because it is a document outlining the internal structure of government rather than a philosophical declaration. It was not designed to be an apologetic of the country's existence as was the Declaration of Independence. The only obvious reference to religion in the U. S. Constitution is the next to last line which reads, "Done in Convention by the Unanimous Consent of the States present the Seventeenth Day of September in the Year of our Lord one thousand seven hundred and Eighty seven and of the Independence of the United States of America the Twelfth." This language simply reflects the common practice of referencing a date as the number of years since Christ. A.D. stands for the Latin phrase, *Anno Domini*, meaning "in the year of the Lord."

The fact that the Framers of the Constitution recognized 1787 as "the year of our Lord," indicates the common acceptance of the calendar based on the life of Jesus Christ. "Our Lord," of course, is a reference to Jesus Christ, but this certainly does not mean that Americans must be Christians or that only Christians can express their religious views in America.

The First Amendment and the Four Freedoms

More specific to this issue is the First Amendment to the Constitution, ratified on December 15, 1791, which says,

> Congress shall make no law respecting an establishment of religion, or prohibiting the free exercise thereof; or abridging the freedom of speech, or of the press; or the right of the

people peaceably to assemble, and to petition the Government for a redress of grievances.

This statement represents the Four Freedoms that all Americans enjoy:

- the freedom of religion
- the freedom of speech and the press
- the freedom to peaceable assembly, and
- the freedom to petition the government

John Leland

The First Freedom mentioned in the Bill of Rights is the Freedom of Religion. Again, "Congress shall make no law respecting an establishment of religion, or prohibiting the free exercise thereof...." Why is religious freedom so important? Why was it the first of the freedoms in the Bill of Rights? What does it really mean? Since so many Americans today think that ministers should stay out of politics, some might be surprised to find that it was none other than a Baptist pastor that was largely responsible for this most important of all freedoms being included in the Bill of Rights.

Historian Joseph Dawson writes, "If the researchers of the world were to be asked who was most responsible for the American guarantee for religious liberty, their prompt reply would be 'James Madison.' However, if James Madison might answer, he would as quickly reply, 'John Leland and the Baptists.'"[128]

Even in the Land of the Free and the Home of the Brave there was considerable religious persecution in colonial America-especially toward the Baptists and Quakers. The original British colonies had established tax-supported Christian denominations. Most were Anglican, Congregational or Presbyterian. All three practiced infant baptism and abhorred those who did not. The "Anabaptists" (which meant re-baptizers) were a persecuted lot from day one. Baptists have never believed that infants should be baptized, and because these Baptist forefathers held to believer's baptism, they were arrested, imprisoned, fined, whipped, banished and had their property confiscated. All these things took place here in America, the land of the free and the home of the brave.[129]

Before the Massachusetts Bay Colony was 20 years old, with Congregationalism as the official church, laws were passed against the Baptists. One said,

> It is ordered and agreed, that if any person or persons, within this jurisdiction, shall either openly condemn or oppose the baptizing of infants, or go about secretly to seduce others from the approbation or use thereof, or shall purposely depart the congregation at the ministration of the ordinance ... after due time and means of conviction-every such person or persons shall be sentenced to banishment.[130]

As a result of this law, Pastor Roger Williams was banished from colonial civilization and had to live among the Native Americans. He fared well, however, and took his punishment as a call from God to evangelize them. You could say Williams was the first "home missionary." Eventually, Roger Williams went to the wilderness area that is now the state of Rhode Island and established a colony that had no state-supported church. The name of the town was Providence. In 1638, he established the a Baptist church. By 1663, Rhode Island was legally established as a colony and had its own constitution that contained one of America's first declarations of religious liberty. The Preamble states:

> We, the people of the State of Rhode Island and Providence Plantations, grateful to Almighty God for the civil and religious liberty which He hath so long permitted us to enjoy, and looking to Him for a blessing upon our endeavors to secure and to transmit the same, unimpaired, to succeeding generations, do ordain and establish this Constitution of government.

By the end of the American Revolution, a Baptist pastor named John Leland was serving a church in Virginia. During his 17-year ministry, Leland baptized over 1,200 converts to Christianity. Leland was not only a powerful preacher, he was also an influential public figure and frequently preached on political issues. The U.S. Constitution, as originally adopted, did not specifically prohibit religious persecution in America though President Washington believed that this was one of the main principles of the Revolution. Nevertheless, Leland feared that if President Washington ever left office, religious persecution by the state-supported denominations would resume without a clear prohibition of it in the Constitution. Therefore, Leland chose to run for political office.

His opponent in the race for the Virginia seat in the House of Representatives was James Madison. Madison was the favorite in the race, but could not win without the support of the Baptists, a large voting bloc. After a long meeting between the two candidates in which Madison agreed to push for a religious liberty amendment, Leland dropped out of the race and gave his support to Madison. The Baptist churches rallied their support behind Madison too, and he was elected.

On the first day of Madison's service in Congress, he stated, "It cannot be a secret to the gentlemen of this House that ... there is a great number of our constituents who are dissatisfied with the Constitution."[131] Madison introduced ten proposed amendments that came to be known as the Bill of Rights. The freedom of religion came chiefly from the influence of John Leland and the Baptists of Virginia. "Congress shall make no law respecting an establishment of religion, or prohibiting the free exercise thereof ..." Had Pastor Leland just kept quiet and not fought in the political arena for religious freedom, America might very well today have state-sanctioned denominational churches similar to the Church of England. You and I would not be free to worship as we do, and our tax dollars would go to support of the state churches. Americans owe a great debt to freedom fighter/pastor, John Leland.

Church and State

Abraham Lincoln

Without the four freedoms that the Constitution preserved, America would not be the leader of the free world today. In the era of monarchies and dynasties, 18th century framers of the Constitution sought to create something entirely new and different. As the great American President Abraham Lincoln later said, "Four score and seven years ago our fathers brought forth on this continent, a new nation, conceived in liberty, and dedicated to the proposition that all men are created equal ... That this nation, under God (emphasis added), shall have a new birth of freedom – and that government of the people, by the people, for the people, shall not perish from the earth."[132]

Abraham Lincoln, a man who was not afraid to bring his Christian faith into the world of politics, warned his fellow Americans of becoming so full of self-reliance that God is forgotten in the public square. On March 30, 1867, Lincoln issued a "Proclamation Appointing a National Day of Fasting." He wrote:

> We have been the recipients of the choicest bounties of Heaven. We have been preserved these many years in peace and prosperity. We have grown in numbers, wealth and power as no other nation has ever grown. But we have forgotten God. We have forgotten the gracious Hand which preserved us in peace, and multiplied and enriched and strengthened us; and we have vainly imagined, in the deceitfulness of our hearts, that all these blessings were produced by some superior wisdom and virtue of our own. Intoxicated with unbroken success, we have become too self-sufficient to feel the necessity of redeeming and preserving grace, too proud to pray to the God that made us! (emphasis added) It behooves us then to humble ourselves before the offended Power, to confess our national sins and to pray for clemency and forgiveness.

Lincolns' words are extremely fitting for America in the 21st century as well as they were in the 19th century. Actually, those words are fitting for all generations, for it was to the ancient Hebrews, that the prophet said, "If my people, which are called by my name, will

106

humble themselves and pray and seek my face and turn from their wicked ways, then will I hear from heaven and will forgive their sin and will heal their land," II Chronicles 7:14.

Dietrich Bonhoeffer

During the rise to power of perhaps the world's most notorious dictator, Adolph Hitler, there existed a lack of involvement in the political realm by the churches of Germany that reminds me somewhat of the lack of involvement going on in the American churches today. When 14-year-old Dietrich Bonhoeffer, the son of a distinguished Berlin physician, announced his intentions to become a pastor and theologian, his brother scoffed at such a foolish idea and said the church is weak, silly, irrelevant and unworthy of a young man's lifelong commitment. To this accusation, Bonhoeffer replied, "If the church is really what you say it is, then I shall have to reform it."

After completing his university studies in Germany, Bonhoeffer was invited to complete his theological training at Union Theological Seminary in New York in the 1930's. He found the American seminary to be sub-par and said, "At this liberal seminary, the students sneer at the fundamentalists in America, when all the while the fundamentalists know far more of the truth and grace, mercy and judgment of God."

As Hitler and the Nazi party rose to power, it became evident that the Lutheran churches had to either oppose Hitler's clearly unbiblical government or acquiesce to it. Most of the German churches chose the easier road and conformed to Nazi theology. Many simply looked the other way and reasoned that they were supposed to be concerned with spiritual things, and not political things. While millions of Jews were being exterminated, German pastors were silent about the slaughter (much as many American pastors today are silent about the slaughter of the unborn).

Church and State

Although the German Evangelical Church welcomed Hitler's rise to power in 1933, Bonhoeffer elected to oppose the Nazi theology and led the rebellion known as the Confessing Church. In "The Church and the Jewish Question" (1933), Bonhoeffer pledged to fight political injustice. "The Nazi injustice must not go unquestioned, and the victims of this injustice must not go unaided, regardless of their religion," Bonhoeffer wrote.[133] In August 1937, the regime announced the Himmler Decree, which declared the training and examination of Confessing ministry candidates (the ministerial students that Bonhoeffer had been secretly training) illegal.

Over time, it became clear to Bonhoeffer and his co-patriots that Hitler could not be stopped militarily and had no intention of granting religious freedom to the subjects of his new world order. They knew that Germany had only one true *Fuehrer* (leader) and that was Jesus Christ, not Adolph Hitler. In a letter to a friend, Bonhoeffer wrote, "Christ is looking down at us and asking whether there is anyone who still confesses him." I believe Christ is asking the same question of us today.

In 1943, Bonhoeffer joined with several high ranking Nazi officials to secretly plan an assassination of Hitler. The plot was discovered, and Bonhoeffer spent two years in a Gestapo prison. He had an opportunity to escape but refused to leave out of fear of reprisal toward his family. He did not know that his brother had been executed, and his brother-in-law, both secret partners in the anti-Hitler movement, had been arrested by the Nazis. Bonhoeffer was removed from the prison and taken to Flossenburg, the Buchenwald concentration camp in the Bavarian forest. On April 9, 1945, three weeks before American forces liberated Flossenburg, he was executed. Today the tree from which he was hanged bears a plaque with only ten words inscribed on it: *Dietrich Bonhoeffer, a witness to Jesus Christ among his brethren.*[134]

Martin Niemöller

Another German Christian pastor who sought to be salt and light in the public square of Nazi Germany was Martin Niemöller. Niemöller was a decorated U-boat captain for Germany in World War I, but left the military to become a minister prior to WWII. In the 1930's, Niemöller was an outspoken opponent to Nazi theology and a leader of the *Bekennende Kirche* (The Confessing Church). He was a principal leader behind the Barmen Declaration that criticized the politics of Hitler and the acquiescence of the Christian church in Germany.[135] For his dissidence, Niemöller was arrested by the Nazis in July of 1937 and remained in a concentration camp throughout the war. Niemöller survived the war and later travelled the world to speak of the atrocities that occurred under Hitler and to warn the people of God of the dangers of looking the other way when politics goes awry. Niemöller is famous for the following statement:

> *First they came for the socialists, and I did not speak out because I was not a socialist.*
>
> *Then they came for the trade unionists, and I did not speak out because I was not a trade unionist.*
>
> *Then they came for the Jews, and I did not speak out because I was not a Jew.*
>
> *Then they came for me, and there was no one left to speak for me.*[136]

At the risk of sounding like an alarmist, I believe that America in the early part of the 21st century is not entirely unlike pre-Nazi Germany. We have a weak church backbone in this country. Our churches are filled with people who do not study the Bible and live by its principles. As I've highlighted in previous chapters, we have a largely superficial church in this country that is suffering from the same biblical ignorance and moral depravity as those outside of the church.

Church and State

I also see a pervasive false theology among American churches known as the Prosperity Gospel, which is really no Gospel at all. This is the notion that God wants to make all of us healthy and wealthy, but it is clearly unbiblical and of the world. It is a teaching that draws big crowds with "itching ears," however. You can really a fill up a room if you have entertaining music and visual displays, and then preach a sermon that is really more of a "pep talk" on how to be blessed by God. I'd like to ask the Apostle Paul if he just didn't have enough faith, when he spent most of his ministry in a filthy Roman jail cell, and what he thinks about the Prosperity Gospel.

Pastors that are so seeker-sensitive that they will not preach the truth of the Bible on the days' moral and political issues, often out of a fear that they will turn off the crowds who come to their churches, are like the demons in the man of the Gerasenes: they are legion (Mark 5). Whenever I have spoken in public against the push for legalization of homosexuality and abortion, I've seen members of the clergy who advocate in favor of these sins.

There is no shortage of clergy in this country who cannot see, or do not want to see, the dangerous philosophy of our current governmental leadership. If the current congress gives legal amnesty to the 30 million illegal aliens in this country, they could literally vote themselves into permanent power. Mr. Obama has already demonstrated his lack of respect for human life (through his abortion policies), and his disdain for Christians who oppose such policies (through his support of hate crimes legislation, the Employment Non-Discrimination Act, the Freedom of Choice Act, the repeal of the Defense of Marriage Act, his repeated public speeches disavowing the Christian heritage of this nation, and the appointment of radical anti-Christian governmental officers). If the 2010 census, which he moved under the control of his White House Chief of Staff by the way, enables him to redistrict the country, God only knows what kind of power grabs the administration could make.

On a local level, I speak frequently around the state of Tennessee on these issues. I always like to ask the crowd, "How many of you knew, before today, that Tennessee has the most liberal constitutional protections for abortion of any state in the U.S.?" Routinely, less than 5% of the pastors in the room are aware. In our state government, there is not one single representative, from all the church denominations, present to lobby the government on behalf of religious and moral principles. Why not?

I mentioned previously that the confessing churches of Germany issued the Barmen Declaration to formally oppose the political and moral principles of the Nazi movement. In a similar vein, many American religious leaders signed a document recently called the Manhattan Declaration.[137]

Martin Luther King, Jr.

If we fast-forward a few decades from the time of Bonhoeffer and Niemöller, we find another "Luther" of deep Christian faith who chose to be salt and light in the public square. Dr. Martin Luther King, Jr. was a relatively unknown Baptist preacher born in Atlanta, Georgia. As the pastor of a black Baptist church in Montgomery, Alabama, King entered the national spotlight when he led the 1955 Montgomery Bus Boycott and was instrumental in forming and leading the Southern Christian Leadership Conference. In 1963, King led a march on Washington over civil rights and delivered the famous "I Have a Dream" speech on the steps of the Lincoln Memorial. Unfortunately, King's outspokenness brought him enemies – as was true of other faithful prophets like Jeremiah, Isaiah, Amos, John the Baptist, and Jesus. An assassin silenced King at the young age of 39, but his example and influence lives on.

It would have been easy for King to spend his career as a preacher involving himself only with the affairs of the church and its congregation. He didn't have to speak out about racial and social injustice, and King would have likely lived a much longer life had he kept to himself and stayed out of politics. In Dr. King's last Sunday sermon, before his assassination, the great reformer said:

On some positions, cowardice asks the question, is it expedient? And then expedience comes along and asks the question – is it politic? Vanity asks the question – is it popular? Conscience asks the question is it right? And there comes a time when one must take a position that is neither safe, nor politic, nor popular—but must take it because it is right.[138]

When you think about Christians being involved in the arena of politics and government, many have the notion that the church should just focus on preaching the Gospel and leading people to follow Christ. Certainly, this is the fundamental work of the church, but God calls the church to stand for righteousness and justice in the public square as well. As I asked in the introduction to this section of the book: Why is there no slavery in America today like there was in the early 1800's? Is it because more people have become Christians than in the early 1800's? No. Has slavery gone away because more people listen to preaching on the radio, the internet, television and in print today than they did in the early 1800's? No. Actually, the only reason that people don't own slaves in America today is that godly men pushed to have the laws changed. It is the responsibility of Christians to push for legislation that protects the innocent and upholds righteousness.

The prophet Amos had some pretty radical words of condemnation for the church in his day, and I think these words could apply to many American churches today as well. Listen:

Seek good, not evil, that you may live. Then the Lord God Almighty will be with you, just as you say he is. Hate evil, love good; maintain justice in the courts. Perhaps the Lord god Almighty will have mercy on the remnant of Joseph. Therefore this is what the Lord the Lord God almighty, says . . .

"I hate, I despise your religious feasts; I cannot stand your assemblies . . . Away with the noise of your songs! I will not listen to the music of your harps. But let justice roll on like a river, righteousness like a never-failing stream!"

Could it be that when God looks down upon the American churches, he says "I hate, I despise your stadium-like worship services, your Christian concerts, your cruises with Christian celebrities ... because you ignore the 50 million babies that have been slaughtered in the womb, you looked the other way when the courts ruled Bible reading and prayer in schools unconstitutional, and you grossly mock my righteous standards as you legislatively foster divorce, extra-marital sex, pornography and homosexuality?" God help us.

Section Two
How to Be Salt and Light

By now, I hope that I have convinced you that it is not only morally right for American Christians to get involved in the public square as salt of the earth and light of the world, it is absolutely essential to the salvation of our country. But I want to do more than persuade you to think correctly about these matters. I want to motivate you to take action. There are many realistic and practical things that we can do to turn our country around, but they all involve "doing" something. "Do not merely listen to the word, and so deceive yourselves. Do what it says," warns God's word in James 1:22. The next five chapters will show you things that we, and our churches, can do to exalt righteousness in this nation. We'll see that ...

Chapter Six

Christians Must Legislate Morality

"The great, vital, and conservative element in our [political] system is the belief of our people in the pure doctrines and the divine truths of the Gospel of Jesus Christ."[139]

U.S. CONGRESS, 1854

Church and State

Hear the words of President Garfield:

> Now more than ever before, the people are responsible for the character of their Congress. If that body be ignorant, reckless and corrupt, it is because the people tolerate ignorance, recklessness and corruption. If it be intelligent, brave and pure, it is because the people demand these high qualities to represent them in the national legislature ... if the next centennial does not find us a great nation ... it will be because those who represent the enterprise, the culture, and the morality of the nation do not aid in controlling the political forces.   U. S. President James Garfield, 1876.[140]

Some people say that the church should stay out of politics because "you can't legislate morality." Perhaps they use this line of reasoning to justify their passivity in the realm of law and government. Many pastors in America refuse to preach on controversial political subjects that the Bible addresses, or help their congregations be aware of these issues in the public square, because they think that "you can't legislate morality," so they focus on evangelism and other important functions of the Christian church!

I humbly beg to differ. All laws legislate morality! That is what legislation does. Legislation says "X behavior is wrong, and it is punishable by law." Sir William Blackstone, the legal expert whose writings greatly influenced the founders of our country, argued that the task of the legal system is to command what is right and prohibit what is wrong.[141] For instance, the law says that killing an innocent person is wrong and it is punishable by law: this is a moral judgment. If the law didn't "legislate morality," then people would commit murder and get away with it. Then we would not have a society; we would have bedlam. As I said in a previous chapter, the only reason that Americans don't still own slaves is because godly citizens pushed and pushed until slavery was declared illegal in the 13th amendment to the U.S. Constitution. If we would do the same thing over pornography, abortion, etc., we might see those things become a thing of the past too.

If a nation does not legislate morality, it tends to legitimize immorality by default. What proponents of "you can't legislate morality" usually mean is that legislation cannot make a person be good: that is quite true. Legislation can, however, punish a person for doing wrong, and this is the biblical function of government according to the Bible in Romans 13:1 - 5: Verses one and four say:

> Everyone must submit himself to the governing authorities, for there is no authority except that which God has established. The authorities that exist have been established by God ... For he (the magistrate) is God's servant to do you good. But if you do wrong, be afraid, for he does not bear the sword for nothing. He is God's servant (*diakonos*), an agent of wrath to bring punishment on the wrongdoer.

Only a society that does legislate morality can survive, and without the revelation of the light of Scripture, legislation will become senseless and ineffective. Proverbs 29:18 says: "Where there is no revelation, the people cast off restraint; but blessed is he who keeps the law." This was often the case during Israel's wandering periods in the OT. A common refrain in the OT is "In those days Israel had no king; everyone did as he saw fit" (Judges 17:6). Time and again, the nation of Israel wandered away from God and his moral code because her leaders did not toe the line. How true is that today of America? Many of our national leaders are afraid of professing their faith in Christ and adherence to the Bible, because nobody wants to be seen as "politically incorrect," so we call evil, good and good, evil. We have called the gruesome murder of an innocent child "good," and we call preaching the truth about such things as "evil." God help us!

If our government does not say, "Right is right and wrong is wrong," enlightened by biblical truth, God may let us end up living in a state of anarchy. So, governments must legislate morality.

Church and State

Whose morality will be legislated?

You see the real question is not whether the government should legislate morality. The real question is "Whose morality will the U. S. government legislate?" Until the last 60 years or so, that was easy to answer. The laws of the United States have been essentially biblical laws for the majority of American history. I believe that is a primary reason that America grew to such a state of prominence among the nations of the world in such a short time. For hundreds of years, American children were taught biblical principles and allowed to pray in our public schools. The Ten Commandments were the bedrock of our legal system, and Christianity was the commonly understood religion of America. The result was that America had a good, law-abiding society that was morally healthy, industrious, and successful.

But since the 1950's, this country has gradually loosened itself from the moorings of biblical truth and has slipped off into the dark and dangerous waters of moral relativism. Until the church speaks out against this unholy drift, and Christians start using their privilege of voting to elect Godly men and women into public office, the ship is great danger of sinking.

The first Chief Justice of the United States Supreme Court, John Jay, wrote, "Providence has given to our people the choice of their rulers, and it is the duty, as well as the privilege and interest of our Christian nation to select and prefer Christians for their rulers." As you probably know, America is not mentioned in the Bible, and we have no guarantee from God that He will protect us and keep us safe. If we do not return to the biblical values that made us a great nation, we will soon self-destruct! Let me share with you some examples of modern Christians trying to make a difference in the public square.

Eric Schumacher, pastor of Northbrook Baptist Church in Cedar Rapids, Iowa, said he has contacted his legislators and has urged his congregation to do the same regarding the legalization of "same sex" marriage in that state. "[A]s citizens in a 'government of the people, by the people, and for the people,' we have both the privilege and the responsibility to act so that our civil government functions as God intended -- to approve what is good and to punish what is bad," he told Baptist Press. "To neglect participation in such a government is to squander a privilege that few Christians have enjoyed in church history."[142]

A Christian attorney in Springfield, MO, Dee Wampler, has taken appropriate action to reverse the national trend of doing away with "Christmas holidays" by calling them "Winter holidays." Wampler compiled information on every school calendar in Missouri. He found only seven school systems within 100 miles of Springfield that did not recognize Christmas. In each of those towns, he contacted local pastors and recruited volunteers to attend school board meetings and petition to put Christmas back on the calendar. This kind of action is perfectly legal, under the First Amendment, and it is perfectly Christ-like for churches to come together in support of an historical holiday.

Due to the engagement of Mr. Wampler, six of the seven school systems changed the calendars back to Christmas Holidays! Some boards said it was an inadvertent mistake, while others had close votes about the change, but now the students in those six schools have a school calendar that reflects the holiday for what it is: a Christmas holiday.

Worries about lawsuits were the main reason there was opposition to the name change, but Wampler said that's unfounded. "There has never, ever been a recorded case in history that says you can't recognize Christmas on the calendar," the attorney said. The one school that elected to keep "winter holidays," has dug in their heels, and Wampler continues to address their board of education. "Perseverance is the key," he said. "You have to stay after them."[143]

Thoughts on Contacting Elected Officials

Many times Christians are surprised to find out that a phone call, letter or e-mail is warmly received by elected officials. Most

Church and State

elected officials are asked to make decisions on more bills than they can really take time to read and study. This is why lobbyists and engaged citizens can be so helpful. When legislators are asked to vote on over one hundred bills in a week, especially toward the end of the session calendar, it is very helpful for them to hear from knowledgeable citizens on the various issues. A respectfully written letter or e-mail, advocating for a position without calling them names or maligning their character, can actually have a significant effect on the outcome of a bill in consideration. Legislators get a lot of automated mail, usually from political action committees and groups pushing a particular cause, so a personal letter or e-mail from a constituent can really rise to the top of the mail stack.

When calling or writing an elected official, please keep the following points in mind:

1. Address them properly and spell their name correctly. You can get this information from various government web sites.

2. Make sure you have the bill or resolution number and names correct, i.e.: HB0312 or SJR0127.

3. Be sure to give your name, address and a phone number if requested, and explain that you are a resident of the area the legislator represents. You don't have to live in an elected official's district for them to listen, but it will be more effective if you do.

4. Keep your comments brief and to the point. If calling, write down a statement that you want to make and keep it to a sentence or two. Most likely, a secretary or intern will take your call and write down what you have to say, so keep it short and to-the-point.

5. Always be respectful even if you totally disagree with everything for which they stand. Jesus said, "Do to others as you would have them do to you." Remember, honey catches more flies than vinegar.

Rallies and Public Hearings

As there is a growing movement throughout the United States to redefine our laws in ways that approve of homosexual relationships, abortion, banning Bible studies and Ten Commandments displays, etc., it is incumbent upon Christians to have a proper response to those who advocate for these positions in the public square. These battles are being waged in the media, and many times state and local governments will hold public hearings so that citizens can speak on issues with lots of news reporters and cameras present to capture it all. Frequently, Christians respond to these opportunities in one of two ineffective ways: apathy or anger. I'll address apathy first, because it is the most common response.

In spite of the fact that those who believe in traditional marriage are in the vast majority, time and time again the biblical institution of marriage has been legislatively redefined by a minority of homosexual activists simply because the body of Christ has chosen to ignore the situation and not show up.

Even though most people think that killing an unborn baby is wrong, when a public hearing is held on the matter, pro-life advocates are frequently in the minority. This is especially true with Christian pastors. Being a pastor myself, I have often been the only pastor present to testify to the truth in a county commission meeting or city council hearing. In Matthew 5:13-16, Jesus likened his followers to salt and light and explained that if the salt loses its saltiness and the light is hidden under a bowl, the world will not know of the love and truth of God. Far too often, Christians have not been engaged in these debates, for a variety of reasons, and this has given the minority activists carte blanche to pass laws that undermine the family, which is the foundation of our society.

The second ineffective response of Christians is anger. While it is understandable that believers sense moral outrage at the behavior of corrupt or at least misguided politicians, Christians must follow Christ's example of loving the sinner, but rejecting the sin. Loving the sinner means showing courtesy, respect, kindness, mercy, and having compassion for the suffering that has been caused by the sin. Loving the sinner DOES NOT MEAN calling them names, losing your temper, getting into a shouting match or other kinds of altercations. NEVER PHYSICALLY ASSAULT SOMEONE IN THE NAME OF CHRIST OR THE BIBLE. Even though Jesus was angry at the commercialism he witnessed in the Jerusalem temple (Matthew 21), he did not physically assault or harm anyone.

Though we should strive to love the person caught up in sin, we must not pretend that we approve of their choices. It is not "loving" to let a person think that God approves of behavior that is clearly sinful and self-destructive. Not loving the sin means that we recognize the individual is caught up in a sinful lifestyle or mindset that is causing pain, and helping him or her see that Christ offers a way out of this lifestyle is the redemptive approach.

Of course, many people today have no concept of sin and really don't think that their behavior is sinful. If I say to the homosexual activist, "I love you in Christ, but I hate your homosexuality because it is sin," he may not understand that statement at all. To him, being a homosexual is not a choice; he believes he was born that way, and he'll probably take offense at my suggestion that how he thinks he was created by God is somehow sinful. Even though we may not be able to convince the advocate that our intentions are well meaning, we can be respectful and show them compassion as a fellow human being and creation of God.

"Don't impose your values on me, man. It's a free country!"

One more thing must be considered when the Christian seeks to pass legislation enforcing biblical values. How do you respond to the argument that says: "You can have your Christian values for your life, but don't try to impose them on me." At first blush, this argument sounds reasonable doesn't it? As I've said before, most Christians don't like to argue and when somebody says this, we tend to back off.

122

But let's unpack that argument some and see the faulty line of reasoning.

To say that it is wrong for Christians to impose their values, legislatively, on people who may not share those values, the arguer ignores several realities about law and a just society.

1. A just society is ruled by law, rather than men. This means that a law applies to all members of the society, even if some of them don't agree with the law. For instance, we have laws that punish drivers who are intoxicated, even if they have caused no one any harm by their drunken driving. Most Americans probably agree that it is best to have laws against drunk driving, but there are some people who like to go out and get drunk and then drive home. They think that they are capable of driving safely and as long as they don't wreck their car or hurt anyone else, they've done nothing wrong.

If we bought the argument that it is wrong for the majority to impose their laws on the minority who disagree, then the drunk driving prohibition would only apply to those who do not drink and drive? Those who do drink and drive, the ones most likely to kill themselves or others, would be exempt from punishment. So it is in everyone's best interest that the laws against drunk driving apply to everyone, regardless of whether or not they agree with the law.

2. All ideas are not of equal worth. It is a false idea to think that all moral positions are of equal validity. For example, the homosexual activist would argue that his or her version of love is equally valid as the traditional love between a man and woman. He says that it is just as wrong for Christians to prevent him from marrying his male partner as it would be for him to prevent a heterosexual from marrying his female partner. All of this is based on an *a priori* line of reasoning that holds all ideas are equally valid.

But this simply is not true. For example, the child molester may think that what he does to innocent children is good in his warped sense of morality. The law enforcement officer who arrests the child molester thinks the abuse of children is wrong. Who is right? If both moral positions are equally valid, then nobody can say one is right and the other is wrong. A society that doesn't punish wrong behavior will quickly degenerate into utter chaos. So it is necessary for those who know the truth to impose that truth on those who do not know the truth. That may seem harsh and unfair, but this is why we pass laws to keep people from drinking and driving, or from stealing, or committing murder, rape, child abuse, etc. A just society must punish evil.

3. It is false to think that freedom means being free to do as you please. Sometimes people will claim, "It's a free country; I can do whatever I want." Well, actually, you cannot do whatever you want in a "free country." You cannot murder your parents, you cannot abuse your wife, you cannot steal from the grocery store, you cannot drive 100 miles per hour through your neighborhood, etc. The only reason that we have a free country is that our laws keep us from doing self-destructive things and from doing things that hurt others.

With all of this in mind, we follow the admonition of II Timothy 2:23-26, "The Lord's servant must not quarrel; instead, he must be kind to everyone, able to teach, not resentful. Those who oppose him he must gently instruct, in the hope that God will grant them repentance leading them to a knowledge of the truth."

Chapter Seven

Christians Must Know and Share the Truth

"If I profess with the loudest voice and clearest exposition every portion of the truth of God except precisely that little point which the world and the devil are at that moment attacking, I am not confessing Christ, however boldly I may be professing Christ. Where the battle rages, there the loyalty of the soldier is proved, and to be steady on all the battlefield besides, is mere flight and disgrace if he flinches at that point"[144]

MARTIN LUTHER, FOUNDER OF LUTHERANISM

Church and State

In John 8:32, Jesus said: "You shall know the truth, and the truth shall set you free."

There are many issues threatening the family, traditional morality and religious liberty in the U.S. I wish I could cover all of the most important threats to the family and give you an historical, logical and biblical defense for each issue, but I don't want this book to look like a dictionary and weight ten pounds. Other authors have addressed the details of issues like abortion, homosexuality, pornography, divorce, etc., and I don't intend to make this book focused on issues.

Unfortunately, many of the people who sit in the pews of American churches each Sunday do not possess a biblical worldview, at least not on moral/political subjects. As a result, they see the moral problems of this nation through the darkened eyes of the world rather than the light of scripture.

As a pastor who is also involved in a public policy organization, I walk the awkward line between religion and politics that most Christians do not wish to cross. I preach the whole counsel of God each Sunday in my church, and I speak to pastors and church leaders on a regular basis about informing their congregations on ways to be involved in the public square. Most pastors will preach on cultural and moral issues from time to time, but few have equipped their church members to become engaged in any real, meaningful way.

At the Family Action Council of Tennessee, we encourage churches to form Salt and Light Ministries (a.k.a. Ethics and Public Affairs, Moral Concerns or Community Impact Committees) that give the church members ways to be salt and light in the public square on an on-going basis. For instance, we encourage committees to conduct periodic voter registration drives. If these are done on a monthly or quarterly basis, they don't appear to be aimed at getting some candidate elected. It is surprising to know how many Christians are not registered to vote, and providing copies of the state registration form at a table in the church foyer occasionally, is a simple way to improve this.

Another helpful task of a Salt and Light Committee is to educate the church on legislative issues and mobilize them to speak to their representatives. Many Christians don't know about the moral perils we are facing in government, and most have never contacted their elected officials. Many never think about it, because they just ignore the political realm altogether, but some are simply uninformed and a little fearful of the idea of talking to a mayor, governor or legislator.

To tell you the truth, communicating with elected officials is really easy and very effective. There are lots of good web sites that allow you to enter your zip code and then send a pre-written e-mail or letter to your legislators on a given issue. If you simply want to contact them on your own, you can search by their name on the internet and find their legislative web site where they accept messages. Focus on the Family has a helpful web site (www.citizenlink.com), and the Family Research Council maintains a similar one (www.frc.org/action), where you can register to receive e-mail alerts when your input is needed on a matter in Washington D.C. You can also find the state-level family policy council in your state from the Citizenlink.com web site. Of course, if you live in Tennessee, visit www.FACTn.org.

While sending an email or a letter is very helpful, all elected officials accept phone calls from their constituents as well. This is where some people might be a little nervous, but there is no reason to be afraid. First of all, you almost never actually talk to the politician when you call. Most likely you'll either just leave a voice mail or you'll leave a message with a secretary or an intern. <u>FEAR NOT: Most political staff members will not argue with you in person.</u> Their job is to simply record your concern and pass it along to the legislator. Even if you happen to contact him or her in person, he or she will usually express gratitude for your call even if not agreeing with your position. It is extremely rare for a politician to be unpleasant or argumentative with a constituent, unless – of course – the constituent is rude and abusive. All politicians realize that they need their constituents to like them and think they are listening, so feel free to call, visit or contact them any way that is practical. Just remember to be like Christ at all times!

The main thing is to contact them. Most politicians never hear from their constituents on anything outside of some personal issue or request. Honestly, when a state legislator gets a dozen or so phone calls or e-mails on a topic, he or she will pay attention. Sometimes only one personal contact can make a difference, especially if he or she is on the fence. When you contact them, please be respectful and courteous, speaking to others as you would have them speak to you. Again, the main thing is to contact them.

Helping the Church become Informed

I suppose that one of the biggest challenges we face in getting the body of Christ to be salt and light in the public square is helping the church become informed and knowledgeable. If Christians don't know there is a problem, they will never think of contacting their elected officials. As the prophet Hosea lamented, "My people are destroyed for lack of knowledge" (Hosea 4:6). Unfortunately, many pastors refuse to share information on these issues with their congregation, but that doesn't mean the people in the pew have to remain uninformed.

I see two very correctable problems in this area: poor communication networks among Christians and an unbiblical worldview. As I say, these are both easily correctable, but they do require some effort. Let me address each specifically.

Improving Communication among Christians

Erich Bridges, writing for *Baptist Press*, in an article titled, "What would our world be like without newspapers?" made an interesting statement about the deluge of information that Americans get:

> "Water, water, everywhere, nor any drop to drink." High school kids used to memorize that line from Coleridge's "The Rime of the Ancient Mariner." In the poem, sailors go mad with thirst under a scorching sun as their cursed vessel sits, day after day, "idle as a painted ship upon a painted ocean." Thirsty in the midst of an ocean: Sounds like our relationship to the ever-increasing torrent of information flooding us from every direction. We can't even begin to absorb it, much less use it effectively.[145]

> Information workers, who comprise about 63 percent of the U.S. workforce, are each bombarded with 1.6 gigabytes of information on average every day through e-mails, reports, blogs, text messages, calls and more," writes Andrea Coombes of *The Wall Street Journal.* "The average knowledge worker —from computer programmers and rocket scientists to administrative assistants and accounting clerks — spends about 25 percent of the day searching for needed information, getting back to work after an interruption and dealing with other effects of information overload.[146]

I can certainly agree with this. There is so much happening in the world that it is a little overwhelming. I get daily e-mails from the Ethics and Religion Liberty Commission of the SBC, Baptist Press, Focus on the Family, the Eagle Forum, Family Research Council, Coalition for Working Families, etc., and it can become too much to take in, but think about the alternative. What if we knew nothing about God's work around the world and never heard the truth?

I dare say that most American Christians get all their news from two sources: the local evening television news (ABC, CBS and NBC affiliates) and their local city newspaper.

I hate to burst your bubble, but if you rely on your local city newspaper, or the big three television news networks, for your information, you are usually hearing only the liberal side of a story. If you rely on a national newspaper, you are probably hearing an even more biased one-sided story than you would get on the television. Let me give you an example to illustrate my point.

Church and State

In August 2009, the ELCA (Evangelical Lutheran Church in America) held its annual convention in Minneapolis, MN. According to the ELCA's printed convention schedule, the 5th session of the convention was to begin at 2:00 PM on August 19. The most controversial item of the session was: "Consideration: Proposed Social Statement on Human Sexuality." Among the issues to be debated was whether practicing homosexuality is a behavior that should disqualify a person from the pastoral ministry. An eyewitness described what happened outside during this scheduled session:

> This curious tornado touches down just south of downtown and follows 35W straight towards the city center. It crosses I-94. It is now downtown. The time: 2 PM. The first buildings on the downtown side of I-94 are the Minneapolis Convention Center and Central Lutheran. The tornado severely damages the convention center roof, shreds the tents, breaks off the steeple of Central Lutheran, splits what's left of the steeple in two...and then lifts (Baptist Press email).

In spite of this obvious (at least to me) warning of God's judgment on the denominational misdirection, the convention voted to approve homosexual clergy. I believe that if a tornado ripped the steeple off of a church where I was about to vote to affirm the kind of sin that caused God to destroy Sodom and Gomorrah with fire from Heaven, I would have gotten out of there as fast as I could. The 1,045 delegates voted by a 2/3 majority to lift the ban on homosexual clergy.

I first read about this warning of God in Baptist Press. The Tennessean, my local newspaper for Nashville, reported the decision in the August 21st edition, but said nothing whatsoever about the tornado. That night, ABC Evening News also reported the vote on TV but said nothing of the tornado. USA Today ran an AP story on the convention, and only mentioned the tornado briefly at the bottom of their coverage, stating: "Wednesday's debate was interrupted briefly in the afternoon when severe storms and a possible tornado passed through downtown Minneapolis, damaging the steeple of an ELCA church across the street from the convention center. Delegates were allowed to remain in the convention hall, but a few jokes about God's wrath proved inevitable. 'We trust that the weather is not a commentary on our work,' said the Rev. Steven Loy, who was helping oversee the convention."

One thing that I have noticed for several years now is the fact that news and information related to Christian faith and values is almost completely ignored in both the television and print news media unless some celebrity TV pastor is caught doing something illegal or immoral. Think about this for a minute: when was the last time you saw a pastor interviewed on the TV news for his take on issues of the day? Does that idea seem strange and foreign to you? There was a time in this country when the pastors were the only educated men in society and what they had to say, on all matters, was listened to carefully. In the early years of this country, pastors were the leaders of the community and their sermons gave people guidance in all areas of life: remember, God's word addresses all of life because God cares about the whole person. Today, pastors have to purchase on-air time on a religious cable channel in order to be heard.

Think about the nightly fare of sitcoms on TV: when was the last time you saw a functional, healthy Christian family portrayed that attends church, reads their Bible and prays? In other words, what television character looks like you? When was the last time you saw a normal, everyday Christian American portrayed in a movie out of Hollywood? Except to poke fun at religious people, the film/television industry wants to make us think that normal Christian families don't even exist. I can't think of one network television show today, aside from the religion channels and paid preaching programs, that has an obviously Christian character on it, much less a pastor, can you? A recent review of television networks found that one out of every four television shows has a homosexual character and he/she is always portrayed in a positive light. Do you see the bias?

Whenever I pick-up a copy of the local city newspapers and scan for anything related to the church or Christian faith, it is usually an article by a liberal minister promoting some unbiblical teaching. If you only read the local newspapers, you'd think that Christians conservatives are a bunch of ignorant bigots who go around beating their wives, trying to shoot homosexuals and take away women's rights. A few months ago, during the TN General Assembly debate over abortion, there were five articles on the same page about the topic. One article was from a conservative Christian, pro-life legislator, and the other four were from pro-abortion advocates, including the newspapers' own editorial: 4 to 1. How is that supposed to be fair and balanced coverage? If the local evening news and newspaper is the only news source that Christians are getting, we see why we have a real problem.

In John 8:32, Jesus calls us to "know the truth." We cannot be set free from lies unless we know the truth. One of the most important ways of knowing the truth, aside from reading the Scriptures, is to read Christian newspapers, magazines, and on-line/e-mail based newsletters. At least that way, you get to hear both sides of the story. It takes work to be informed. It is much easier just to watch the tube or read the tabloids in the grocery store, but I implore you to spend the extra time and money to subscribe to Christian news magazines, e-newsletters, and biblical television programming.

Form a Salt and Light Ministry in your church

Many churches have flower committees, potluck planning committees, decorating committees, etc. Why not have a committee whose purpose is to study moral and cultural issues and inform the congregation on such matters? At the Family Action Council of Tennessee, we call these "Salt and Light Ministries," but they might be called Moral Concerns Committees, Ethics and Public Affairs Teams, etc. I've written a manual for churches to use in creating such a ministry. It is called Salt & Light Ministry Handbook for Churches (see www.Eight32Publishing.com).

The following are some recommendations on forming a Salt and Light Committee:

I strongly urge church members to request the approval of the church's pastor and/or designated leadership before beginning a "Salt & Light Committee." Also, it is critical that this committee be non-partisan and follow the rules of the Internal Revenue Service (see www.FACTn.org/resources for more ideas).

1. Prayerfully identify like-minded members of your congregation to work together to keep your congregation informed about issues in the public square. In almost every congregation, of any size, God has placed some members of the body who care about social and political causes. Many times, these people are longing to find a way to use their passion and knowledge to help the congregation be salt and light in the public square.

2. Regularly ask your church to pray for their elected officials.

3. Download and distribute church bulletin inserts, posters and other leaflets that inform the congregation of issues in the public square.

4. Encourage your church members to subscribe to e-mails and newsletters that cover federal and state legislative issues from a Christian perspective. If the church members don't know the truth about the issues, how can they speak out?

5. Conduct letter and phone campaigns to legislators, voter registration drives, candidate forums, etc. For information on conducting a voter registration drive, see www.ivotevalues.org.

6. Enroll church members in Christian worldview training, using Focus on the Family's "The Truth Project," a DVD-based curriculum (see www.truthproject.org).

7. Submit factual articles and letters to the editor of your local newspapers. You don't have to make up all the content: most Christian political involvement groups are happy for you to copy and paste their facts and talking points into letters to the editor of your local paper.

8. Help develop and promote the use of legislative candidate surveys during election cycles. As long as they are strictly non-partisan and do

not grade or recommend candidates and parties, voter guides have been found to be compliant with IRS guidelines.

9. Keep your pastor informed about IRS regulations on pastoral and church political activities. The IRS actually gives the clergy more freedom than many assume. This information is readily available on the internet at sites like www.alliancedefensefund.org.

10. Support and promote events like Ministers' Day on the Hill, Legislative Prayer Breakfasts, See You at the Pole, Sanctity of Human Life Sunday, Religious Freedom Sunday, National Day of Prayer, etc.

11. Encourage and promote patriotic church services to which candidates for office and elected officials can be invited. As long as you invite candidates from both parties, there is nothing in the law or Internal Revenue Code that prevents churches from allowing candidates to speak on the issues or their faith.

12. Assign members of the committee to monitor certain news and informational websites to check for additional information about which the church should know, particularly local issues with which state and national organizations might not cover. If you have enough members of your committee, you could assign different issues to different members for monitoring and research. As I mentioned, I've produced a Salt & Light Ministry Handbook that is available through www.Eight32Publishing.com.

Helping the Church Develop a Biblical Worldview

Why did Jesus come into the world? Many things come to mind with that question. We might answer, "To save us from our sins," or "to die on the cross," or "to fulfill God's plan of salvation," and all of those are good and right answers. Did you know, however, that Jesus answered that question for us? In John 18:37, Jesus was interrogated by Pontius Pilate before his crucifixion, and he said:

In fact, for this reason I was born, and for this I came into the world, <u>to testify to the truth</u>. Everyone on the side of truth listens to me.

Dr. Del Tackett, author of Focus on the Family's "The Truth Project," says:

> Here is one of the clearest and most objective statements that Jesus made about the reason He came into the world. This statement doesn't override the others, in fact, I think it helps to clarify many of them. For example, in 1 John 3:8, we are told that Jesus came to destroy the works of the devil. What is the devil? A liar. When Jesus said that He didn't come to bring peace, but a sword, we understand that it is not a worldly sword that He is referring to. The Scripture makes reference over and over again to the sword being the Word of God (Eph 6:17), which in Hebrews 4:12 reiterates that it divides (" *For the word of God is living and active. Sharper than any double-edged sword, it penetrates even to dividing soul and spirit, joints and marrow; it judges the thoughts and attitudes of the heart.*") This reinforces what Jesus said about coming for judgment that the blind should see (John 9:39), coming as a light (John 12:46), came to preach (Mark 1:38), came to give us understanding so that we would know him who is true (1 John 5:20), and so on (visit www.TheTruthProject.org).

To Jesus' statement about testifying to the truth, Pontius Pilate sarcastically asked, "What is truth?" Del Tackett would say, "Correspondence to reality. Truth is that which is really real." God is truth and without God, we could not know the truth.

Jesus came into the world to "testify to the truth." Earlier, Jesus told his followers, "I am the way, the truth and the life" Jn. 14:6. <u>There really is such a thing as absolute truth</u>, in spite of the fact that Satan has deceived the world into thinking that there is no such thing as truth. How badly do we need to know the truth in our world today?

Many people in modern America have come to the conclusion that there is no such thing as absolute truth. "Truth is in the eye of the beholder," some would say. In fact, it's kind of funny that people would say that because to say that there is no such thing as absolute truth is to make an absolute truth claim. In other words, to declare that "There is no such thing as absolute truth" is to say that your belief is absolutely true, which is a contradiction.

We all know, intuitively, that there is truth and then there are lies, the opposite of truth. For example, if it is raining outside, I can truthfully say "It is raining outside." Reality supports my truth claim, and only the insane (those who do not perceive reality) would say that I am lying. If it is raining outside, but you cannot see or hear the rain, then you are faced with a dilemma: believe that I am telling you the truth about the rain or assume that I am lying. If I tell you it is raining outside, when it is actually not raining outside, I have lied to you and eventually reality will prove my falsehood.

The question for mankind today, then, is not so much: "Is there such a thing as absolute truth?" but "What is the truth?" Christians know that God, as revealed through His Son Jesus Christ, is the truth, and when we witness about Christ, we are telling the truth to a world that would not see or hear the truth otherwise.

I have a friend who volunteers with a ministry called the Christian Women's Job Corps. She worked with a woman named Monique. This ministry pairs spiritually mature Christian women with poor women who need job skills and mentoring. As my friend began to mentor and minister to Monique, soon Monique came to know the truth about Jesus Christ and she surrendered her life Christ as Lord. The truth sets people free! As a result of the ministry of my friend, Monique began living the life of a Christian, but her troubles were not over.

After Monique began to live for Christ, a family member falsely accused her of a crime and reported it to the police. Although Monique was innocent and the truth was on her side, she was still arrested and spent seven days in jail. In time, Monique was found to be innocent and was exonerated of all charges against her. The truth won out! Just as Satan is called "the accuser of the brethren," in

Scripture, sinful people often will accuse Christians of sin out of mere hatred toward God. Satan used the false children of Abraham, in John 8, to accuse Jesus of all manner of sin and wrong doing, and Satan will accuse us of evil too.

What would have happened to Monique if the truth had not come out? She might have spent years in jail paying for a crime that she did not commit. That is why it is so important that we know the truth![147]

The World Has Been Deceived

If you read through any newspaper, you'll see evidence of the deception and brokenness that sin brings to the human heart: murder, crime, drug abuse, corruption, divorce, adultery, violence, death, etc. There is a cosmic battle in this world that has been raging for thousands of years. It is not a battle between criminals and police or a battle between America and terrorists or a battle between Democrats and Republicans. All those battles are merely symptoms of this larger, cosmic battle that is being waged in the hearts and minds of men. It is a cosmic battle between truth and lies.

"In this corner, weighing in at 250 pounds, is Jesus Christ: King of kings, Lord of lords, the Way, the Truth and the Life!"

"In the other corner, weighing in as a 95-pound weakling, is Satan, the deceiver, the accuser of the brethren, and the father of lies."

The prize in this contest is not a golden belt or a flashy trophy: it is the salvation of mankind throughout all eternity. God is fighting for us, but we are so easily besieged and fooled by the lies of the devil. Consider Adam and Eve in the Garden of Eden (Genesis 1-3).

In the Garden of Eden, God gave Adam and Eve one rule: stay away from the Tree of Knowledge of Good and Evil! This was no fuzzy, unclear boundary. God warned them that if they eat of that tree they would surely die. So what did Satan do? Did he try to strong-arm

Church and State

Adam and Eve and force the apple down their throats? No, he lied to them ... and they swallowed the lie: hook, line and sinker. In chapter three, verses one through five, Satan questioned Eve and suggested that what she heard God say was not true and that God wouldn't do what he promised. Satan always casts doubt on God's word and gets us to question God. That is his most powerful weapon: doubt. As you know from the story, Eve began to doubt God's word, and decided she knew better than God, so she disobeyed the Lord and opened the door for sin to infect all of creation.

If truth is what is really real, then the lie is the absence of reality or insanity. If you visit a facility for the severely mentally ill, you might find a patient who says, "I am Jesus Christ." This man might sincerely believe that he is the Lord, but he is wrong. He is out of touch with reality because he has believed something that is not true as though it were. "Do not be deceived," Paul says in Galatians 6:7-8, "God cannot be mocked. A man reaps what he sows. The one who sows to please his sinful nature, from that nature will reap destruction; the one who sows to please the Spirit, from the Spirit will reap eternal life." There is no way to get around it: Satan lies to us and deceives us into doubting God, and the result is always pain and suffering.

They say that the best way to spot a counterfeit bill is to be so familiar with the real thing that you immediately spot a fake. I'd say that the best way to spot a counterfeit "truth claim" is to be so familiar with the Truth (from God and his word) that when you hear a lie of Satan you will immediately recognize it and dismiss it.

On a recent Wednesday night, we heard gunshots out in the street in front of my church during Prayer Meeting. There were some young people in the duplexes across the street involved in an altercation and many of us saw one of them walking around with a shotgun. At the end of the evening, we found out that two people had been shot and drugs were involved. Now somebody is sitting in jail, or worse, all because he or she "believed" that those drugs and illegal gain would make him or her happy.

Recently the former Titans football star, Steve McNair, was killed by his 20-something year old mistress. Satan fooled him into thinking that he would be happier with her than being with his wife and children.

People make terrible decisions all the time because they are lied to and deceived. That is why Jesus came into this world: to testify to the truth. Then he entrusted the truth with us, his followers, and instructed us to go into all the world and teach His truth to the lost (see Matthew 28:18-20).

Our world today is not much different than it has always been. This cosmic battle between the Truth and lies has been raging since day one. In the Old Testament era, the prophet Isaiah lamented:

> Surely the arm of the Lord is not too short to save, nor his ear too dull to hear. But your iniquities have separated you from your God; your sins have hidden his face from you, so that he will not hear. Is. 59:1-2

How did things get in such bad shape? You ask. Read on . . .

> So justice is driven back and righteousness stands at a distance; truth has stumbled in the streets; honesty cannot enter. Truth is nowhere to be found, and whoever shuns evil becomes a prey. Is. 59:14-15

So if the truth is hidden and is nowhere to be found, then mankind cannot know right from wrong. If the world does not hear the truth, how will they know that they need a Savior? This is why the church must not only know the Truth, but we must share it with the world.

The Church Must Know the Truth and Share it with the World

Romans 12:2 says, "Do not conform any longer to the pattern of this world, but be transformed by the renewing of your mind. Then you will be able to test and approve what God's will is – his good, pleasing and perfect will." How can a lost and dying world know the difference between the truth and a lie, right and wrong, safety and danger, salvation and damnation? By "renewing the mind," Paul answers.

What does it mean to "renew the mind?" I think it means to fill your mind with so much truth that all the lies bubble up to the surface and disappear into thin air. Imagine that you had a bottle of carbonated soda and you began to pour motor oil into the bottle. Motor oil is heavier than soda pop, so the oil would sink to the bottom of the bottle. If you keep pouring the oil in, eventually all the soda pop will overflow out of the top of the bottle and the bottle will be full of oil.

The same process happens as we fill our minds with the truth of God's word. In addition to reading the Bible nearly every day, I like to read Christian newspapers every week. I also subscribe to a few Christian news magazines. I get a bunch of Christian news e-mails every day, and I love to listen to Christian talk radio. I've read hundreds of Christian books too. I know you are thinking that I am just weird, but let me tell you: if you don't transform and renew your mind with God's truth, you will fall for the lies of Satan.

Colossians 2:8 warns, "See to it that no one takes you captive through hollow and deceptive philosophy, which depends on human tradition and the basic principles of this world rather than on Christ." I've already discussed how the false idea of a "constitutional separation of church and state" has taken captive the minds of millions of American Christians, but false ideas are pervasive among Christians in many areas.

National polls have shown, for several years, that Christians are just as immoral as non-Christians in many areas. Extra-marital sex, adultery, divorce, child abuse, alcoholism, pornography, etc. are moral cancers that infect the churches as well as the rest of society. In one national survey, it was found that only about 8% of people who regularly attend the church could be described as holding a biblical worldview. The truth is that the church has been taken captive, mentally, by Satan. Either we don't know the truth or we don't believe it. Either way, God's truth needs to renew our minds.

Let me challenge you with an experiment. For one week, turn off the television at home, and spend the time you normally would spend watching TV either reading the Bible or reading Christian books or listening to Christian radio. I guarantee you that by the end of the week, you will be a different person than you are today. You'll see things more from Christ's perspective, and you will have a deeper love for God and appreciation for your salvation.

If your church does not have a Biblical Worldview curriculum, consider using The Truth Project. I have trained hundreds of church leaders in Tennessee to use The Truth Project, and God is doing a tremendous work through this curriculum worldwide. Learn more at www.TheTruthProject.org.

Chapter Eight

Christians Must Elect Christian Leaders

"In selecting men for office, let principle be your guide ... look to his character ... When a citizen gives his suffrage [vote] to a man of known immorality he abuses his trust; he sacrifices not only his own interest, but that of his neighbor, he betrays the interest of his country."[148]

NOAH WEBSTER

"The God of Israel spoke, the Rock of Israel said to me: 'When one rules over men in righteousness, when he rules in the fear of God, he is like the light of morning at sunrise on a cloudless morning, like the brightness after rain that brings the grass from the earth.'"

II SAMUEL 23:3-4

The American Founding Father, Noah Webster, said: "In selecting men for office, let principle be your guide … look to his character … When a citizen gives his suffrage (vote) to a man of known immorality he abuses his trust; he sacrifices not only his own interest, but that of his neighbor, he betrays the interest of his country."[149] Since millions of voting-age Americans have not been raised with a biblical worldview, it is not surprising that we continually elect politicians who are pro-abortion, pro-homosexuality, pro-gambling, anti-religious liberty, etc.

Dr. James Dobson adds: "half the Christians in America aren't even registered to vote, and of those who are, only half go to the polls." According to the U.S. Census Bureau, as many as 25-35% of the voting age population is not even registered to vote. That translates to between 45 and 65 million Americans! What is worse is that Census Bureau statistics also show that only 53% of Americans who were eligible to vote did so in 2000, and only 39.3% voted in 2002. It would be safe to say that less than half of all professing Christians vote in any given election.

Here's more sobering news: Many believers fail to consider their biblical values when voting, often choosing candidates whose positions are at odds with their own beliefs, convictions, and values. A recent study by the Pew Forum on Religion and Public Life shows that about half of Americans say moral values have little to do with their voting decisions.[150]

As I mentioned earlier, Christians must understand that all authority belongs to God. As Romans 13 explains, the magistrate, or ruler, is the *diakonos*, or servant/minister, of God. The authority that the ruler holds is actually God's authority, and God has delegated that authority to him for the good of the people. Even what we do in the ballot box, by casting a vote for a candidate or an ordinance, proposition or amendment, is exercising our God-given, delegated authority. Therefore, we are stewards of that authority and must exercise it as such. Politics, for the believer, should not be about gaining power or beating the other party or candidate; it should be about good stewardship of God's delegated authority.

In Matthew 25, Jesus gave us the parable of the talents. In the story, a wealthy landowner was leaving for a long trip, so he called three of his servants together and gave each of them a "talent." The talent can represent almost anything: money, ability, etc. As the story goes, two of the servants displayed good stewardship of what they had been given. They used their gifts and multiplied them. The other servant, out of fear, buried his talent in the ground. When the master returned to settle his accounts, he praised and rewarded the good stewardship of the first two servants, but he scolded the slothfulness of the third. As punishment, the master took away the talent that had been entrusted to the "lazy, wicked servant," and sent him away.

For our purposes in this book, consider what if the talent, with which we have been entrusted, is the ability to vote for those who rule over us? If we think of the vote as a talent, I ask you, "How have we, as American Christians, stewarded our voting?" Have we been faithful to steward the delegated power of the vote well, by examining the candidates and voting for those who share our biblical values, or have we mismanaged the talent by voting for those who look good on the outside, but have no biblical and moral guidance on the inside? What is worse: have we been lazy and wicked with our talent by burying it in the ground, i.e. not even being registered to vote? If so, should we be surprised if one day we have the right to vote taken away from us all together, as the wicked, lazy servant lost even the one talent that he had?

Dwight D. Eisenhower, the 34th President of the United States said, "The future of this republic is in the hands of the American voter." Samuel Adams, in 1781, said, "Let each citizen remember at the moment he is offering his VOTE...that he is executing one of the most solemn trusts in human society for which he is accountable to God and his Country." Daniel Webster, the great statesman of the early 19th century said, "Our destruction, if it comes at all, will be from ... the inattention of the people to the concerns of their government, from their carelessness and negligence." In the 2008 Presidential elections, 122 million Americans voted, but 108 million did not. There are an estimated 60 million evangelical Christians in this country, yet in the November 2008 presidential election, some 38 million Christians did not vote.[151] Would God not be justified in taking away our talent (voting ability) and allowing us to live under a dictatorship?

Rev. Charles Finney, a powerful preacher who was responsible for thousands coming to Christ through revival meetings in the early years of our Republic, wrote these convicting words:

> The Church must take right ground in regard to politics ... [T]he time has come that Christians must vote for honest men and take consistent ground in politics ... Christians have been exceedingly guilty in this matter. But the time has come when they must act differently ... God cannot sustain this free and blessed country which we love and pray for unless the Church will take right ground ... It seems sometimes as if the foundations of the nation are becoming rotten, and Christians seem to act as if they think God does not see what they do in politics. But I tell you He does see it, and He will bless or curse this nation according to the course [Christians] take [in politics].[152]

This was written in 1830! How much more do we need to heed these words today? Please remember, for the Christian, politics is not about getting power and beating the other party. Partisan philosophy changes like the wind. There was a time in this country when the national Democratic Party stood for the mainstream, traditional values of religious Americans. For some reason, over the last several decades, the party, at least at the federal level, has come to represent more of the values of the far-left (supporting things like abortion, same-sex marriage, pornography, separation of church and state, etc.) This doesn't mean that today's Democrats are all bad and Republicans are all good either. There are plenty of moral policy problems within the Republican Party too, and there are some outstanding Christians in the Democratic Party. This is why believers need to examine each candidate and each issue before casting their votes. For the Christian, politics is really about the obedience to the cultural mandate of Jesus in Matthew 5:13-16: it is about being the salt of the earth and light of the world. It is about standing up for righteousness and justice, calling a sin, a sin, and doing something about it.

"But the people who know their God shall stand firm and take action." Daniel 11:32

Get Involved

I saw a bumper sticker on a car the other day that said: "Get involved! The world is run by people who show up!" There is a lot of truth to that statement. How many times do we see our elected officials do terrible things and lament that they just don't seem to get it? Well, maybe the problem is that there are no good people willing to serve. We must get involved.

Chapter Nine

Christians Must Clean House at Home

[W]e have no government armed with power capable of contending with human passions unbridled by morality and religion . . . Our Constitution was made only for a moral and religious people. It is wholly inadequate to the government of any other.[153]

PRESIDENT JOHN ADAMS

All societies of men must be governed in some way or other. The less they have of stringent state government, the more they must have of individual self-government...

Men, in a word, must necessarily be controlled either by a power within them, or a power without them; either by the word of God, or by the strong arm of man; either by the Bible or by the bayonet.[154]

ROBERT WINTHROP, U.S. SPEAKER OF HOUSE, 1847-49

Church and State

The photograph was invented in 1839, and within a few short years, pornography began to circulate through the American culture. Pornography comes from the Greek word, *porneia*, meaning "sexual immorality," and it is translated in the New Testament in Jesus' Beatitudes (Matthew 5:32) and in Jesus' discourse on divorce in Matthew 19:9 as "unfaithfulness".

Largely due to the enormous circulation of Hugh Hefner's *Playboy Magazine* since 1953 (which, by the way, is worth an estimated five billion dollars), print and internet pornography is the single most destructive force against the family in America. In the 1990's, the domain name, business.com, was sold for a record seven 7.5 million dollars, but the domain, sex.com, was valued at sixty five million dollars! One author has suggested, "Perhaps we should call it the inter*course*net instead of the internet, as an estimated twenty eight thousand people every second, mostly men (seventy-two percent) but also women (twenty-eight percent), view pornography. Every thirty-nine minutes a new pornographic video is created in the United States."[155]

Christians Aren't Immune to the Ravages of Sexual Sin

When surveyed, fifty-three percent of men who attended Promise Keeper rallies confessed that they viewed pornography that week. More than forty-five percent of Christians admit that pornography is a major problem in their home. An anonymous survey conducted recently by the web site, www.Pastors.com reported that fifty-four percent of pastors admitted viewing porn within the last year. In an online newsletter, thirty-four percent of female readers of *Today's Christian Woman* admitted to intentionally accessing Internet porn. One out of every six women who read the magazine report that they struggle with addiction to pornography[156]

In the 1964 case, *Jacobellis v. Ohio*, late Supreme Court Justice Potter Stewart wrote in his concurring opinion, "I shall not today attempt further to define the kinds of material I understand to be [hardcore pornography] ... But I know it when I see it...." If the Supreme Court knows it when they see it, why can't they outlaw it, and why can't the church get rid of it?

Partially, the reason that the Church is no more pure than the rest of society is that Christians today are inundated with sexual media through television and movies. Look at these statistics that were reported by the Parents' Television Council:

• Seventy percent of all shows have sexual content, up from fifty-six percent in the first study in 1998 and sixty-four percent in 2002.
• Among the top twenty most-watched shows by teens, seventy percent include some kind of sexual content, and nearly half (forty-five percent) included some amount of sexual behavior.
• Among shows with any sexual content involving teen characters, just under one in four (twenty-three percent) include a reference to sexual risks or responsibilities.
• Nearly eleven thousand expletives were aired during primetime on broadcast TV in 2007 — nearly twice as many as in 1998.
• The f-word aired only one time on primetime broadcast TV in all of 1998 — yet it appeared one thousand, one hundred, forty-seven times on the television in 2007 on one hundred, eighty-four different television broadcast programs.

• In 2007, fifty-two percent of the programs that contained the f-word and fifty-five percent of the programs that contained the s-word aired during the 8:00 p.m. "family hour."

What is the result of this sex-saturated media consumption on American youth? Forty-six percent of high school students in the United States have had sexual intercourse, and one case of a sexually transmitted disease is diagnosed for every four sexually-active teens. [157]

I Peter 5:8-9 says:

Be self-controlled and alert. Your enemy the devil prowls around like a roaring lion looking for someone to devour. Resist him, standing firm in the faith, because you know that your brothers throughout the world are undergoing the same kind of sufferings.

Satan is seeking whom he may devour

There is no doubt that Satan can devour a life. Look at all of the people in America who are addicted to smoking and dying of lung cancer, and all the people addicted to alcohol, and other kinds of drugs, whose lives have been devoured. Look at all the people whose families have been destroyed by pre-marital sex, adultery and divorce, and all the careers that have been ruined because of stealing, cheating and lying. Think of all the hurting people in psychiatric hospitals and recovery centers; all the people wasting away in our nation's prison system; all the victims of drunk driving, murder, rape, etc. There is no doubt about it. Satan can devour and destroy a life.

Who is the Devil? The Hebrew word, *Satan*, is used three times in the Old Testament:

- I Chronicles 21: Satan tempts and incites King David into disobeying God and taking a census of the people
- Job 1-2: Satan is in the heavenly court and is an accuser of Job and questions Job's loyalty to God
- Zechariah 3: Satan also stands before the heavenly court to accuse Joshua the High Priest.

In the New Testament, Satan (Hebrew) is translated into the Greek as *diabolos*. This word is translated into the English language as *Devil*. All these names mean the same thing: "accuser or slanderer of mankind." In the New Testament, he is also called "Beelzebub, prince of demons," (Matthew 12), "Belial," (II Corinthians 6), "dragon," "ancient serpent," "enemy," "evil one," "god of this world," "prince of the power of the air," "ruler of this world," and "the tempter."

In the late 1960's, Flip Wilson made famous the phrase, "The devil made me do it." This notion that Satan is no longer a permanent resident of the heavenly council but is actually an independent evil power that rules a demonic kingdom on earth is really not found in the Old Testament. During the 400-year inter-testamental period, some of the books of the Apocrypha and the dualistic writings of the Zoroastrian religion in Persia gave Satan this role more so than Hebrew Scriptures. The New Testament gives us a clearer picture of Satan's role in the world today.

The Top Ten works of Satan in the world:

1. He brought sin into the world (Genesis 3, II Corinthians 11)

2. He tried to tempt Jesus (Matthew 4)

3. He tempted Judas into betraying Jesus and committing suicide (John 13)

4. He murders and lies (John 8, Revelation 12)

5. He disguises himself as an "angel of light" (II Corinthians 11)

6. He distracts unbelievers from hearing the gospel (Luke 8 and II Cor. 4)

7. He oppresses humankind (Acts 10)

8. He causes illness (Luke 13, II Corinthians 12)

9. He has the power to kill unbelievers (Hebrews 2, I Cor. 5) but cannot kill a believer (I John chs. 4 and 5)

10. He tries to lure Christians into sin and ineffectiveness for God (Eph. 4, I Tim. 3, II Tim. 2, I Peter 5, and I Thess. 2)

Let's camp out for a moment on this last one. In Ephesians 4:27, the Bible says "And do not give the devil a foothold." In I Timothy 3:7, Paul teaches that a pastor/minister and a deacon "must also have a good reputation with outsiders, so that he will not fall into disgrace and into the devil's trap."

In II Timothy 2:24-26, again Paul teaches ministers and other church leaders how to handle criticism and conflict in the church saying: "And the Lord's servant must not quarrel; instead, he must be kind to everyone, able to teach, not resentful. Those who oppose him he must gently instruct, in the hope that God will grant them repentance leading them to a knowledge of the truth, and that they will come to their senses and escape from the trap of the devil, who has taken them captive to do his will." In I Thessalonians 2:18, Paul is writing that he wanted to come back and visit the church in Thessalonica . . . "For we wanted to come to you—certainly I, Paul, did, again and again—but Satan stopped us."

We see that Satan is "trying to get a foothold in our lives." That he has set "traps" for Christians to fall into (by getting into trouble outside the church and by not handling criticism and conflict well inside the church), and Satan seeks to prevent us from taking the Gospel to lost people and ministering to others.

So what is a believer to do?

Resist him and stand firm in the faith by keeping the big picture in mind. Remember, Christ came to earth to destroy the work of the devil.

Hebrews 2:14-15 "Since the children have flesh and blood, he too shared in their humanity so that by his death he might destroy him who holds the power of death—that is the devil—and free those who all their lives were held in slavery by their fear of death."

I John 3:8 "He who does what is sinful is of the devil, because the devil has been sinning from the beginning. The reason the Son of God appeared was to destroy the devil's work."

But his work is not yet finished.

I Corinthians 15:20-24 "But Christ has indeed been raised from the dead, the first-fruits of those who have fallen asleep. For since death came through a man, the resurrection of the dead comes also through a man. For as in Adam all die, so in Christ all will be made alive. But each in his own turn: Christ, the first-fruits; then, when he comes, those who belong to him.

Then the end will come, <u>when he hands over the kingdom to God the Father after he has destroyed all dominion, authority and power</u>" (emphasis added).

Revelation 20:7-10: "When the thousand years are over, Satan will be released from his prison and will go out to deceive the nations in the four corners of the earth—Gog and Magog—to gather them for battle. In number they are like the sand on the seashore. They marched across the breadth of the earth and surrounded the camp of God's people, the city he loves. But fire came down from heaven and devoured them. And the devil, who deceived them, was thrown into the lake of burning sulfur, where the beast and the false prophet had been thrown. They will be tormented day and night forever and ever."

In addition to remembering that Christ will one day destroy the work of Satan, Christians must learn to use our spiritual armor. Ephesians 6:10-18 tells us:

[10]Finally, be strong in the Lord and in his mighty power. [11]Put on the full armor of God so that you can take your stand against the devil's schemes. [12]For our struggle is not against flesh and blood, but against the rulers, against the authorities, against the powers of this dark world and against the spiritual forces of evil in the heavenly realms. [13]Therefore put on the full armor of God, so that when the day of evil comes, you may be able to stand your ground, and after you have done everything, to stand. [14]Stand firm then, with the belt of truth buckled around your waist, with the breastplate of righteousness in place, [15]and with your feet fitted with the readiness that comes from the gospel of peace. [16]In addition to all this, take up the shield of faith, with which you can extinguish all the flaming arrows of the evil one. [17]Take the helmet of salvation and the sword of the Spirit, which is the word of God. [18]And pray in the Spirit on all occasions with all kinds of prayers and requests. With this in mind, be alert and always keep on praying for all the saints.

Church and State

CAVEAT

As we talk about cleaning up the house of God, let me make one thing very clear: <u>We cannot wait until our own house is clean before we try to clean up the public square!</u>

In a newspaper interview, a reporter once asked me if Christians have the right to tell non-Christians that they should live moral lives when so many Christians live immoral lives themselves. My reply was "absolutely yes." Even though a physician is sick, he can still prescribe life-saving medicine to others who are sick. Even if a lawyer is corrupt, he can still give his clients good advice on how to obey the law. Even though a state patrolman might drive too fast, he still knows the dangers of reckless driving.

I cannot wait until I have a perfect marriage to stand up and declare that marriage is better than cohabitation, sodomy or polygamy. We cannot wait until every mother in America honestly says that she wants to have her baby before we make the murder of her preborn baby a crime. We cannot wait until there are no more abusive husbands in the body of Christ before we change our "no fault divorce" laws so that most people have to stay married and work out their problems.

I hate to say it, but as long as the church is made up of human beings, we will never be completely sin-free, at least not until Christ comes and takes us home. Even though we have our own problems, we cannot let that stop us from calling sin a sin when we see it in the public square and trying to warn others from sin's dangers.

Chapter Ten

Christians Must Pray for Government

In the beginning of the contest with Great Britain, when we were sensible of danger, we had daily prayers in this room for the divine protection. Our prayers, Sir, were heard; and they were graciously answered. All of us, who were engaged in the struggle, must have observed frequent instances of a superintending Providence in our favor. To that kind Providence we owe this happy opportunity of consulting in peace on the means of establishing our future national felicity.

And have we now forgotten that powerful friend? Or do we imagine we no longer need its assistance? I have lived, Sir, a long time; and the longer I live, the more convincing proofs I see of this truth, that God governs in the affairs of men. And if a sparrow cannot fall to the ground without his notice, is it probable that an empire can rise without his aid?

BENJAMIN FRANKLIN, CONSTITUTIONAL CONVENTION

It behooves us then to humble ourselves before the offended Power, to confess our national sins and to pray for clemency and forgiveness.[158]

PRESIDENT ABRAHAM LINCOLN

Church and State

In January of 2009, several important processes began in both the federal and state levels of government. Many state legislatures convened for the first of two annual sessions. Several new legislators began their service to our states, and many other things in politics changed due to the balance of power shifting from one side to the other in both state and federal legislative bodies. Also in January 2009, a new U.S. President, Barack Hussein Obama, was inaugurated and numerous freshman U.S. Senators and Representatives began their service to our country. Across the nation, thousands of newly elected government officials and newly hired government employees began their term of service alongside thousands more who continue in their respective assignments.

As with all things new, there was an air of excitement and hope in January that things were going to improve in politics now that new people have come to power. The degree to which things will actually change, and the directions in which those changes will occur, remains to be seen, but one thing is certain: God is still on the throne, and he commands his children to pray for those who govern them. In the first century, the Apostle Paul gave the New Testament churches some instructions on how Christians should relate to those in government, and it is important for followers of Christ to heed those instructions today.

> I Timothy 2:1-2 "I urge, then, first of all, that requests, prayers, intercession and thanksgiving be made for everyone – for kings and all those in authority, that we may live peaceful and quiet lives in all godliness and holiness."

Notice that Paul connected the act of Christians praying for members of the government with the result of peaceful and quiet living. This suggests to us that if we want to live in a civil and peaceful society, then we must be faithful to pray for our rulers and lawmakers. Throughout the Bible, God teaches us that when rulers and lawmakers are righteous and just, the people they rule will benefit from it greatly. For example, Proverbs 29:2 says, "When the righteous thrive, the people rejoice; when the wicked rule, the people groan." Proverbs 14:34 declares that, "Righteousness exalts a nation, but sin is a disgrace to any people." So, it behooves the children of God to pray for their elected officials and to encourage those in power to wield that power in righteousness and justice. The following are five suggestions for ways that Christians can pray for their elected leaders. Pray that our leaders will:

1. Govern as leaders who must answer to God, not just voters
2. Be protected from personal sin, particularly that which would compromise their judgment
3. Remember that: "Righteousness exalts a nation..."
4. Put aside partisanship and personal political ambition
5. Promote and defend a culture that values the traditional family, for the sake of the common good

1. Govern as Leaders who are Accountable to God, not Just to Voters

When Moses was called by God to lead the Hebrew nation out of slavery to the Egyptian Pharaoh, he repeatedly faced the dilemma of whether to obey God or to obey the popular will of the people. A review of the story in the Old Testament book of Exodus reveals that Moses suffered great anguish, at times, in seeking to follow the will of God when God's own people pressed him to abandon God's will. Moses was very much a politician in that he represented the people to Pharaoh, made decisions for the benefit of the people, created and enforced laws for the people, and led the people out of the wilderness and into the Promised Land. Just as present day politicians sometimes grapple with the decision whether to do what is right or what is popular, Moses faced this dilemma. It is quite evident that Moses' success as a political leader was largely based on his strong determination to obey God, even when the people did not support him. Consider the following example in the first few chapters of Exodus.

After God came to Moses in the burning bush, God told Moses to go to Pharaoh and demand that the Israelites be released from slavery. Pharaoh, the King of Egypt, was not a man who worshipped

God, and he had no compassion for the Israelite slaves. In fact, Exodus 1:8 reveals what happens when Christians do not get involved in the political process. It says, "Then a new king, who did not know about Joseph, came to power in Egypt." Joseph had been a godly man who served in the government with integrity and the highest of ethics (see his story in Genesis), but now Joseph was dead and evidently no one had taken his place: as a result, Pharaoh made the Israelites his slaves.

When Moses obeyed God's command to go back to Egypt and address Pharaoh, he first checked in with the Israelite leaders.

> In Exodus 4:29-31, the Scripture says: "Moses and Aaron brought together all the elders of the Israelites, and Aaron told them everything the Lord had said to Moses. He also performed the signs before the people, and they believed. And when they heard that the Lord was concerned about them and had seen their misery, they bowed down and worshiped."

So far: so good. Moses, and his assistant, Aaron, had the call of God and the blessings of the people to go to Pharaoh and demand the abolition of Hebrew slavery; but look what happened next. In chapter 5, we read that Pharaoh said "No," and not only that, Pharaoh punished the slaves as a means of inciting them against Moses ... and it worked. In Exodus 5:21, the people turned against Moses and said, "May the Lord look upon you and judge you! You have made us a stench to Pharaoh and his officials and have put a sword in their hand to kill us." Fortunately, Moses was a man of integrity, and he did not cower to the complaints of the people. He went to God, in prayer, and God encouraged him to stay the course, even though the people no longer supported him.

This story is very relevant today, because our form of republican democracy requires politicians to not only be elected by popular votes, but our politicians must be re-elected by popular votes if they are to stay in power. It is very tempting for politicians to cower to the voters and only answer to them when they are called upon to make a difficult decision. Our American forefathers must have known that human nature is such that a man will give in to what is popular if he only fears losing his popularity with the voters. Perhaps that is why many of the original state constitutions required public officials to be believers and men of faith and morals. Politicians who do not fear God, and are only accountable to the voters, are those most easily tempted by the lure of power and money. On the other hand, a man who believes that God has called him to public service, and considers himself ultimately accountable to God, is less likely to vote for something that is wrong just because it happens to be the popular thing to do.

Pray that our government leaders will stand against the tide and do whatever they must do to protect innocent human life, the biblical institutions of marriage and family, biblical morality and religious liberty. Ending abortion, pornography, same-sex marriage, child abuse, prostitution etc. is not a Republican agenda or a Democratic agenda. It is simply the right thing to do, and we must pray that our elected officials will do the right thing — even if it isn't popular.

2. Be Protected from Personal Sin

Another very important thing for us to keep in prayer is that our government officials will be protected from personal sin, especially that which would impede them from making the right decisions. If you watch the evening news or read the newspapers, you cannot help but notice how regularly a government official is accused or convicted of some personal and/or legal transgression. Just recently, we have heard about the Governor of Illinois being accused of trying to sell President Obama's former U.S. Senate seat to the highest bidder. A few months ago, we heard that former presidential and vice-presidential contender John Edwards confessed to marital adultery, even while his wife was out campaigning for him <u>and battling cancer</u>! The Governor of South Carolina, Mark Sanford, has recently confessed to adultery too. I have often thought, in utter frustration, "Can't any good, honest people get elected to office in this country?"

Church and State

God only knows how many good pieces of legislation, or how many life-saving government policies, have never come to realization because good people in public office have gone bad and lost their credibility.

The following statement is credited to Lord John Acton of England who was a writer, publisher and Cambridge University professor during the 19th century: "Power tends to corrupt, and absolute power corrupts absolutely."[159] Politicians are especially prone to corruption due to the power and prestige they possess, and it is essential that Christians pray for them. Proverbs 29:4 says, "By justice a king gives a country stability, but one who is greedy for bribes tears it down." A stable country is one that is ruled by stable, just people. Pray that our new president, all those who serve in Washington, and all those who serve in our state and local governments would be pure and innocent in their personal dealings as well as their public endeavors.

3. Let Righteousness be Sought First

There are many important issues facing our elected officials. The new president has to deal with a struggling economy, the threat of major industries going under, a war in two countries, and continued political unrest all around the world. As of the writing of this book, the state of California is broke and the governor and lawmakers are at their wits end trying to figure out how to keep the state afloat. While all of these matters are important, what is most important is that our leaders govern as godly men and women of integrity. We must not be short-sighted in thinking that as long as the government finds a way to spend money and end wars, everything will all be okay. Remember, the Bible does not say that a strong economy exalts a nation, or that a lack of war exalts a nation or that a low unemployment rate exalts a nation, etc. It says, "Righteousness exalts a nation." You see, righteousness is the most important ingredient in governmental decisions, just as it is in business and personal decisions.

Recently, the most famous and most financially rewarded golfer in history, Tiger Woods, has been in the news. The allegations are that he has been engaged in sexual misconduct and his wife is in the process of divorcing him. As a result of this tarnished image, Woods has lost several lucrative company endorsements and has resigned from the PGA tour. During elections, we always hear the saying "It's the economy stupid!" Unfortunately, people foolishly think that economics are the most important issues in culture. The truth is that the family and person integrity make up the bedrock of our society. Tiger Woods' experience reveals that when the family crumbles, everything else crumbles around it. How I wish voters would see this.

In Matthew 6 Jesus spoke of what is most important in life. He reminded us that God knows we need food to eat, clothes to wear, etc., and that God will provide those things in his time, just as he cares for the birds of the air and the flowers of the field. Listen to Jesus' words in Matthew 6:31-33:

> So do not worry, saying, "What shall we eat?" or "What shall we drink?" or "What shall we wear?" For the pagans run after all these things, and your heavenly Father knows that you need them, But <u>seek first</u> his kingdom and his righteousness, and all these things will be given to you as well.

We must remind our elected leaders that God will bless a nation that is righteous, but he is under no obligation to bless a nation that is evil. God promised Israel, "If you fully obey the Lord your God and carefully follow all his commands I give you today, the Lord your God will set you high above all the nations on earth" (Deuteronomy 28:1). Even though this promise was specifically addressed to Israel, I think it applies to any nation who submits to God's rule.

A nation that murders its children, as Israel occasionally did in pagan worship, cannot expect God's protection. A nation that embraces perversion, like the base homosexuality found in Sodom and Gomorrah, as consistent with God's design for human sexuality, and redefines marriage or undermines it through its divorce laws, cannot expect God's blessings. A nation that teaches its children atheism in the schools and exalts the deity of man, as Babylon did, cannot expect God's continued hand of provision. It is imperative that Christians tell those in elected office that righteousness is what will protect our people better than the most advanced forms of weaponry imaginable.

4. Put Aside Partisanship and Personal Ambition

The fourth prayer request for our elected officials involves the need for them to put aside the traditional partisanship that usually prevails at all levels of politics. I realize that would be a miracle, but I believe in a miracle-working God. When Jesus came on the scene in Jerusalem, he found a Jewish political system that was hopelessly broken through partisan division. Although Jerusalem was under the occupation of the Roman Empire, most of the government was still under the authority of the Jewish leaders. There were no Republicans or Democrats in first century Jerusalem, but there were Pharisees, Sadducees, and Herodians. These politico-religious parties were corrupt, and Jesus exposed their wickedness for all to see. In Matthew 5:20, Jesus said, "For I tell you that unless your righteousness surpasses that of the Pharisees and the teachers of the law, you will certainly not enter the kingdom of heaven."

In Matthew 22, Herodians and Pharisees came together to trap Jesus over the issue of taxation without representation, the same problem that created the surge for American independence from Great Britain over 200 years ago. The Herodians were Hebrews who were loyal to King Herod Antipas and to Roman rule; the Pharisees were opposed to Roman rule, and sought Jewish independence. Both sides thought that by asking Jesus whether or not it was lawful to pay taxes to Caesar, they could trap him in his own words. If he said that paying taxes was wrong, the Herodians would declare him to be instigating tax evasion and bring the Roman authorities after him. If he said paying taxes was good, then the Pharisees would say he was a puppet of Rome, and the Jews should not trust him. Of course, Jesus recognized the trap and sprung it on them instead. The real shame in this story is that all of these parties should have seen Jesus as the long-awaited Messiah and joined him in bringing the nation of Israel together under God. Instead, they were constantly competing with each other and merely saw Jesus as another threat to their political power.

Our political problems in America are not with the Democrats or Republicans, because neither party's positions are all good or all bad and certainly not all those elected under a party label are all good or all bad. Our problem comes when those who make up those parties allow the lust for power to become the goal, instead of just and righteous policies. And the political nastiness only increases when even good and righteous ends become justification for the use of means that are not just or righteous. If power belongs to God, and He bestows it on whomever He will, then grasping for it by any means necessary is wrong.

It is a lesson that King Nebuchadnezzar of Babylon had to learn the hard way. One day as King Nebuchadnezzar walked in his magnificent palace, he said, "Is not this great Babylon, that I have built … by the might of my power, and for the honor of my majesty?" (Daniel 4:30) We are told that "While the word [was] in the king's mouth," God said: "sovereignty has been removed from you." A "spirit of Nebuchadnezzar" that thinks political power is rooted in mankind and can be exercised for personal glory pervades American politics. We need to pray that our elected leaders will not be taken captive by it.[160] We should pray that our presidents, governors, legislators and judges will be able to put aside the usual partisan bickering and somehow come together to do things that will be in everyone's best interest. Doing things in everyone's best interest brings me to my last prayer topic.

5. Promote and Defend the Family

As the family goes, so goes the rest of the nation. If the family deteriorates, the economy and national security will soon deteriorate as well. The disintegration of family life is costing taxpayers a bundle. A report released in April of 2008 put the cost at an annual one hundred, twelve billion dollars, just in the United States alone. "The Taxpayer Costs of Divorce and Unwed Childbearing: First-Ever Estimates for the Nation and All 50 States," was released by four policy and research groups -- Institute for American Values, Georgia Family Council, Institute for Marriage and Public Policy and Families Northwest.

"This study documents for the first time that divorce and unwed childbearing -- besides being bad for children -- are also costing taxpayers a ton of money," said David Blankenhorn, President of the Institute for American Values, in a press release accompanying the report. Marriage is more than a moral or social institution, the study itself observes. It is an economic institution, and when it breaks down the costs for local, state and federal government are very high. The report points to a yearly one hundred, twelve billion dollar price tag -- or over one trillion dollars in the past decade -- which the authors say is a minimum estimate.

The federal government carries the largest burden, seventy, point one billion dollars, followed by thirty three point three billion dollars for states, and eight point five billion dollars at the local level, on average. These costs arise from a variety of sources: increased taxpayer expenditures for anti-poverty programs; criminal justice and education programs; and lower levels of taxes paid by individuals who, as adults, earn less because of reduced opportunities as a result of having been more likely to grow up in poverty.[161]

So it is clearly in everyone's best interest for our government officials to promote and defend a culture that values the traditional family. Pray that our elected officials will learn this and remember this as they make decisions throughout the year.

Christians Must Pray for Government

    I Timothy 2 urges us to "pray for kings and all those in authority." Won't you obey that command and pray for our elected officials? There are many web sites (such as www.citizenlink.org) that explain how to contact government officials, so please write or call your representatives and let them know you are praying for them. Let them know that you are praying that they will:

1. Govern as leaders who must answer to God, not just to voters
2. Be protected from personal sin, particularly that which would compromise their judgment
3. Remember that: "Righteousness exalts a nation..."
4. Put aside partisanship and personal political ambition
5. Promote and defend a culture that values the traditional family, for the sake of the common good

We will all be the better for it.

Conclusion

We Can Make a Difference!

And so, my fellow Americans: ask not what your country can do for you—ask what you can do for your country.[162]

PRESIDENT JOHN F. KENNEDY

The biblical writer of Hebrews urged Christians:

> Therefore, since we are surrounded by such a great cloud of witnesses, let us throw off everything that hinders and the sin that so easily entangles, and let us run with perseverance the race marked out for us. Let us fix our eyes on Jesus, the author and perfecter of our faith, who for the joy set before him endured the cross, scorning its shame, and sat down at the right hand of the throne of God. Consider him who endured such opposition from sinful men, so that you will not grow weary and lose heart. In your struggle against sin, you have not yet resisted to the point of shedding your blood.   Hebrews 12:1-4

As we reviewed Christian history in chapter three of this book, there were times when God allowed his children to undergo tremendous persecution and suffering. They did "resist to the point of shedding blood." It would seem to me that persecution would turn people off to following Christ, but just the opposite actually happens. Miraculously, the church grew larger and stronger during these years of hell on earth. By being the salt of the earth and the light of the world, Christians engaged the public square and proclaimed the Gospel and truth of Christ. Out of this sausage-grinding of Christianity came a church that spread around the world and set millions of captives free through the power of the Way, the Truth and the Life.

Now, it is our turn

I get tearful when I think about the sacrifices that my Christian ancestors paid to be salt and light in the public square. I think about the young mother, Perpetua (A.D. 202), who was not much older than my own daughter. She asked that the Roman executioners wait for her to fix her hair before throwing her to lions because she did not want to meet her Lord looking disheveled. I think about the ninety year-old Bishop, Pothinus, who gladly laid down his life for Christ when it would have been so much easier to denounce Christ to the government and die a natural death of old age. I think about the missionary, Jim Elliot, who was killed by the Ecuadorian natives he came to save. Before his death, Elliot wrote, "He is no fool who gives what he cannot keep to gain what he cannot lose."

I know that I should not, but I fear what sort of culture my children and future grandchildren will face in the years to come. We American Christians have had it easy for so long, and the Church has declined rather than expanded in the last few generations.

I have to confess I also get angry with the apathy and indifference of so many Christians today that seem to be oblivious to the cosmic battle that is raging all around us.

We stand on the shoulders of giants who loved their Lord Jesus Christ more than they loved the pleasures of this world. As the first preacher of the Gospel, Peter proclaimed to the Sanhedrin: "We must obey God rather than men?" Peter was eventually crucified upside-down, but not before he had brought thousands into the faith. Now it is our turn to change the world. If we must suffer loss of fortune, comfort or even life: so be it.

The Pilgrims set sail for America on September 6, 1620, and for two months braved the harsh elements of a storm-tossed sea. After disembarking at Plymouth Rock, they had a prayer service and began building hasty shelters, but unprepared for a harsh New England winter, nearly half of them died before spring from malnutrition, pneumonia and tuberculosis.

The leader of the group, Gov. William Bradford, wrote:

> They cherished a great hope and inward zeal of laying good foundations, or at least of making some way towards it, for the propagation and advance of the gospel of the kingdom of Christ in the remote parts of the world, even though they should be but stepping stones to others in the performance of so great a work.

I don't know what the future holds for America. I hope it includes a genuine reformation of the church that becomes a sweeping revival of righteousness and justice. If we must suffer tremendously for this to come about, then I pray that we, like the early pilgrims, will be faithful to lay a good foundation for future generations ... even if we be but stepping stones to others in the performance of so great a work!

David Shelley, 2010
Tennessee

A. Religion in the 50 State Constitutions

Statements from the fifty state constitutions regarding religion:

1. Alabama (1901) Preamble: We the people of the State of Alabama, invoking the favor and guidance of Almighty God, do ordain and establish the following Constitution ...
2. Alaska (1956) Preamble: We, the people of Alaska, grateful to God and to those who founded our nation and pioneered this great land ...
3. Arizona (1911) Preamble: We, the people of the State of Arizona, grateful to Almighty God for our liberties, do ordain this Constitution ...
4. Arkansas (1874) Preamble: We, the people of the State of Arkansas, grateful to Almighty God for the privilege of choosing our own form of government...
5. California (1879) Preamble: We, the People of the State of California, grateful to Almighty God for our freedom...
6. Colorado (1876) Preamble: We, the people of Colorado, with profound reverence for the Supreme Ruler of Universe ...
7. Connecticut (1818) Preamble: The People of Connecticut, acknowledging with gratitude the good Providence of God in permitting them to enjoy ...
8. Delaware (1897) Preamble: Through Divine Goodness all men have, by nature, the rights of worshipping and serving their Creator according to the dictates of their consciences ...
9. Florida (1885) Preamble: We, the people of the State of Florida, grateful to Almighty God for our constitutional liberty, establish this constitution ...
10. Georgia (1777) Preamble: We, the people of Georgia, relying upon protection and guidance of Almighty God, do ordain and establish this constitution ...
11. Hawaii (1959) Preamble: We, the people of Hawaii, Grateful for Divine Guidance ... Establish this Constitution ...
12. Idaho (1889) Preamble: We, the people of the State of Idaho, grateful to Almighty God for our freedom, to secure its blessings ...
13. Illinois (1870) Preamble: We, the people of the State of Illinois, grateful to Almighty God for the civil , political and religious liberty which He hath so long permitted us to enjoy and looking to Him for a blessing on our endeavors ...
14. Indiana (1851) Preamble: We, the People of the State of Indiana, grateful to Almighty God for the free exercise of the right to choose our form of government ...

15. Iowa (1857) Preamble: We, the People of the State of Iowa, grateful to the Supreme Being for the blessings hitherto enjoyed, and feeling our dependence on Him for a continuation of these blessings, establish this Constitution ...

16. Kansas (1859) Preamble: We, the people of Kansas, grateful to Almighty God for our civil and religious privileges establish this constitution ...

17. Kentucky (1891) Preamble: We, the people of the Commonwealth are grateful to Almighty God for the civil, political and religious liberties ...

18. Louisiana (1921) Preamble: We, the people of the State of Louisiana, grateful to Almighty God for the civil, political and religious liberties we enjoy ...

19. Maine (1820) Preamble: We the People of Maine acknowledging with grateful hearts the goodness of the Sovereign Ruler of the Universe in affording us an opportunity ... and imploring His aid and direction.

20. Maryland (1776) Preamble: We, the people of the state of Maryland, grateful to Almighty God for our civil and religious liberty ...

21. Massachusetts (1780) Preamble: We...the people of Massachusetts, acknowledging with grateful hearts, the goodness of the Great Legislator of the Universe In the course of His Providence, an opportunity and devoutly imploring His direction ...

22. Michigan (1908) Preamble: We, the people of the State of Michigan, grateful to Almighty God for the blessings of freedom, establish this constitution ...

23. Minnesota (1857) Preamble: We, the people of the State of Minnesota, grateful to God for our civil and religious liberty, and desiring to perpetuate its blessings ...

24. Mississippi (1890) Preamble: We, the people of Mississippi in convention assembled, grateful to Almighty God, and invoking His blessing on our work...

25. Missouri (1845) Preamble: We, the people of Missouri, with profound reverence for the Supreme Ruler of the Universe, and grateful for His goodness. Establish this Constitution ...

26. Montana (1889) Preamble: We, the people of Montana, grateful to Almighty God for the blessings of liberty establish this Constitution ...

27. Nebraska (1875) Preamble: We, the people, grateful to Almighty God for our freedom. Establish this Constitution ...

28. Nevada (1864) Preamble: We the people of the State of Nevada, grateful to Almighty God for our freedom, establish this Constitution ...

29. New Hampshire (1792) Part I. Art. I. Sec. V: Every individual has a natural and unalienable right to worship God according to the dictates of his own conscience ...

30. New Jersey (1844) Preamble: We, the people of the State of New Jersey, grateful to Almighty God for civil and religious liberty which He hath so long permitted us to enjoy, and looking to Him for a blessing on our endeavors...

31. New Mexico (1911) Preamble: We, the People of New Mexico, grateful to Almighty God for the blessings of liberty...

32. New York (1846) Preamble: We, the people of the State of New York, grateful to Almighty God for our freedom, in order to secure its blessings ...

33. North Carolina (1868) Preamble: We the people of the State of North Carolina, grateful to Almighty God, the Sovereign Ruler of Nations, for our civil, political, and religious liberties, and acknowledging our dependence upon Him for the continuance of those ...

34. North Dakota (1889) Preamble: We, the people of North Dakota, grateful to Almighty God for the blessings of civil and religious liberty, do ordain ...

35. Ohio (1852) Preamble: We the people of the state of Ohio, grateful to Almighty God for our freedom, to secure its blessings and to promote our common ...

36. Oklahoma (1907) Preamble: Invoking the guidance of Almighty God, in order to secure and perpetuate the blessings of liberty ...

37. Oregon (1857) Bill of Rights, Article I Section 2: All men shall be secure in the Natural right, to worship Almighty God according to the dictates of their consciences ...

38. Pennsylvania (1776) Preamble: We, the people of Pennsylvania, grateful to Almighty God for the blessings of civil and religious liberty, and humbly invoking His guidance ...

39. Rhode Island (1842) Preamble: We the People of the State of Rhode Island grateful to Almighty God for the civil and religious liberty which He hath so long permitted us to enjoy, and looking to Him for a blessing ...

40. South Carolina (1778) Preamble: We, the people of he State of South Carolina grateful to God for our liberties, do ordain and establish this Constitution ...

41. South Dakota (1889) Preamble: We, the people of South Dakota , grateful to Almighty God for our civil and religious liberties ...

42. Tennessee (1796) Art. XI. III: That all men have a natural and indefeasible right to worship Almighty God according to the dictates of their conscience...

43. Texas (1845) Preamble: We the People of the Republic of Texas, acknowledging, with gratitude, the grace and beneficence of God ...

44. Utah (1896) Preamble: Grateful to Almighty God for life and liberty, we establish this Constitution ...

45. Vermont (1777) Preamble: Whereas all government ought to enable the individuals who compose it to enjoy their natural rights, and other blessings which the Author of Existence has bestowed on man ...

46. Virginia (1776) Bill of Rights, XVI: Religion, or the Duty which we owe our Creator, can be directed only by Reason and that it is the mutual duty of all to practice Christian Forbearance, Love and Charity towards each other ...

47. Washington (1889) Preamble: We the People of the State of Washington, grateful to the Supreme Ruler of the Universe for our liberties, do ordain this Constitution ...

48. West Virginia (1872) Preamble: Since through Divine Providence we enjoy the blessings of civil, political and religious liberty, we, the people of West Virginia reaffirm our faith in and constant reliance upon God ...

49. Wisconsin (1848) Preamble: We, the people of Wisconsin, grateful to Almighty God for our freedom, domestic tranquility ...

50. Wyoming (1890) Preamble: We, the people of the State of Wyoming, grateful to God for our civil, political, and religious liberties, establish this constitution ...

B. Letter by Thomas Jefferson

Commenting on the First Amendment, in a private letter to Baptist churches in Connecticut (1802), then President Jefferson wrote:

Gentlemen:

The affectionate sentiments of esteem and approbation which you are so good as to express towards me, on behalf of the Danbury Baptist association, give me the highest satisfaction. My duties dictate a faithful and zealous pursuit of the interests of my constituents, and in proportion as they are persuaded of my fidelity to those duties, the discharge of them becomes more and more pleasing.

Believing with you that religion is a matter which lies solely between Man & his God, that he owes account to none other for his faith or his worship, that the legitimate powers of government reach actions only, and not opinions, I contemplate with sovereign reverence that act of the whole American people which declared that their legislature should "make no law respecting an establishment of religion, or prohibiting the free exercise thereof," thus building a wall of separation between Church and State (emphasis mine). Adhering to this expression of the supreme will of the nation in behalf of the rights of conscience, I shall see with sincere satisfaction the progress of those sentiments which tend to restore to man all his natural rights, convinced he has no natural right in opposition to his social duties.

I reciprocate your kind prayers for the protection and blessing of the common Father and Creator of man, and tender you for yourselves and your religious association, assurances of my high respect & esteem.[163]

Notes

Introduction

[1] June 2007 speech by presidential candidate Obama made available on YouTube.

[2] April 2009 speech by Obama in press conference with President Gul of Turkey.

[3] To learn more about the faith of our founding fathers, visit www.wallbuilders.com.

[4] Ibid., p. 363.

[5] Russell Kirk, The Roots of American Order (Wilmington, DE: ISI Books, 2008), p. 448.

[6] In 1939 Margaret Sanger, founder of what became known as Planned Parenthood of America, launched a campaign known as "the Negro Project," a concerted attempt to build birth-control clinics in black areas across the country. Today, the vast majority of PP clinics are in minority neighborhoods.

[7] Susan A. Cohen, *Abortion and Women of Color: The Bigger Picture* (see http://www.guttmacher.org/pubs/gpr/11/3/gpr110302.html).

[8] See the film, "Maafa 21: Black Genocide in 21st Century America" by Life Dynamics Corporation, Denton, TX, 2009 (www.Maafa21.com).

[9] Obama got 95% of the black vote in 2008, see: http://www.cnn.com/2008/POLITICS/11/04/exit.polls.

[10] The Guttmacher Institute, named after the former Vice-President of the American Eugenics Society and former President of Planned Parenthood, Dr. Alan Guttmacher, found that some 37% of abortions are performed on black women, http://www.guttmacher.org/pubs/gpr/11/3/gpr110302.html. National Black Catholic Congress reports that abortion is the #1 killer of African Americans, http://www.nbccongress.org/features/abortion_silent_no_more_01.asp.

[11] There is even a "National Black Church Initiative" for the Religious Coalition for Reproductive Care, http://www.rcrc.org/programs/blackchurch.cfm.

[12] An average of 18,430 abortions were performed in Tennessee per year between 1992 and 1996, according to statistics reported by the Alan Guttmacher Institute.

Chapter One

[13] "Our Nation, A Product of Christianity," *Springfield Republican*, 1884. *Theodore Roosevelt: The Man as I Knew Him*, Ferdinand Cowle Iglehart, D. D. (New York: The Christian Herald, 1919), pp. 307-311.

[14] Thomas Paine, Common Sense and the Rights of Man (New York: Classics of Liberty Collection, 1992).

[15] Romans 2:14-15.

[16] Thomas Aquinas, Question 94, *Prima Secundae* in Summa Theologiae.

[17] John Calvin, Institutes of the Christians Religion, IV.XX.16.

[18] J. Budziszewski, <u>What We Can't Not Know</u> (Dallas, TX: Spence, 2004), Introduction.

[19] Zogby International Poll, April 15-17, 2004.

[20] Moore, Keith L. and Persaud, T.V.N., The Developing Human: Clinically Oriented Embryology, 6th edition (Philadelphia: W.B. Saunders Co., 1998): 77, 350. According to the Centers for Disease Control and Prevention, 77% of abortions in the United States occur after the heart of the fetus has begun to beat. "Abortion Surveillance—United States, 2000," 52 Morbidity and Mortality Weekly Report (SS-12) Table 7 (Nov. 28, 2003).

[21] The Harris Poll #18, March 3, 2005.

[22] Ibid.

[23] Zogby International Poll, March 10-14, 2006.

[24] Roe v. Wade forbids any law against abortion in the first and second trimester of pregnancy and even after "viability" if the abortion doctor deems the abortion to be necessary to preserve the mother's "health." Roe v. Wade, 410 U.S. 113, 164-165 (1973). "Health" is defined by the Court as "all factors—physical, emotional, psychological, familial, and the woman's age—relevant to the well-being of the patient." Doe v. Bolton, 410 U.S. 179, 192 (1973).

[25] Thomas Jefferson, <u>Letter to Danbury Baptist Association of Connecticut</u> (January 1, 1802).

[26] Dissenting opinion in *Wallace v. Jaffree*, 1985.

[27] John Eidsmoe, <u>Christianity and the Constitution</u> (Grand Rapids, MI: Baker Book House, 1987), 93.

[28] James Madison, <u>Notes of Debates in the Federal Convention</u> (Athens, OH: Ohio University Press, 1985).

[29] Reports of Committees of the House of Representatives made during the first session of the thirty-third Congress (Washington: A. O. P. Nicholson, 1854), pp. 6-9.

[30] See www.alliancedefensefund.org.

[31] See www.irs.gov/charities.

[32] Information obtained from the Alliance Defense Fund and the Family Research Council.

[33] Ibid.

[34] Ibid.

[35] By the way, did you know that adult stem cell research has produced over 70 cures, but embryonic has never produced one? Why do Hollywood celebrities campaign so hard for embryonic research, that kills living human beings, when it has been so unfruitful?

[36] Address to Yale University Medical School, April 2003.

[37] From his inaugural address at the dedication service for the Free University in Amsterdam.

[38] Bishop Harry Jackson, Jr. is the Senior Pastor of Hope Christian Church in Beltsville, Maryland.

[39] See U.S. Census Burea, http://www.census.gov/Press-Release/www/releases/archives/voting/013995.html

[40] Focus on the Family, *Citizen Magazine*, September 2003, "Believers at the ballot box: Election 2000 by the numbers."

[41] Charles G. Finney, Lectures on Revivals of Religion (New York: Fleming H. Revell Company, 1868, first published in 1835), Lecture XV, pp. 281-282.

[42] From a speech delivered at the Mass Free Democratic Convention, Ithaca, N.Y., October 1852.

Chapter Two

[43] American Presidency Project, "Dwight D. Eisenhower: Address Before the Council of the Organization of American States, April 12th, 1953" (at http://www.presidency.ucsb.edu/ws/?pid=9816).

[44] "ACLU unveils big expansion plans for US heartland," David Crary, Associated Press, June 2008.

[45] Letter distributed via the American Family Association e-mail system, written June 17, 2009.

[46] Martin Luther King, Jr. in the speech, "Strength to Love," 1963.

[47] "Congress shall make no law respecting the establishment of religion, nor prohibiting the free exercise thereof."

[48] See www.wallbuilders.com.

[49] John Quincy Adams, The Jubilee of the Constitution, a discourse delivered at the request of the New York Historical Society, on Tuesday, April 30, 1839, reprinted in 1986 Journal of Christian Jurisprudence.Vol.1, p. 6.

[50] See the research of Robert Cord in Separation of Church and State (New York: Lambeth Press, 1982).

[51] Alexis De Tocqueville, Democracy in America (London: Saunders and Otley, 1838), Vol. I, pp. 305-6.

[52] Ibid., Vo. II, p. 144.

[53] Data is based upon telephone interviews conducted by The Barna Group from August through early November 2008 among 3,012 adults.

[54] Hosea 4:6.

[55] Ku Klux Klan.

[56] Alan Sears is president of Alliance Defense Fund, religious liberty legal alliance based in Scottsdale, AZ. This statement originally appeared in an article in *The Arizona Republic*, August 17, 2003.

[57] William Orville Douglas, Zorach v. Clauson, 343 US 306 (1952).

[58] Justice Hugo Black, *Everson v. Board of Education*, 330 U.S. 1, 15-16.

[59] Jane Doe v. Sante Fe Independent School District, Civil Action No. G-95-176 (U.S.D.C.S.D) Texas., 1995 (court transcription of verbal ruling by judge).

[60] *ACLU of Kentucky vs. Mercer County*, 2005.

Chapter Three

[61] American Presidency Project, "Ronald Reagan: Proclamation 5018 – Year of the Bible, 1983, February 3rd, 1983" (http://www.presidency.ucsb.edu/ws/?pid=40728).

[62] Parentheses mine.

[63] Robert H. Bork, Slouching Towards Gomorrah: Modern Liberalism and American Decline (New York: Harper Collins, 1996).

[64] Acts 12:2

[65] Eusebius, Ecclesiastical History, 2:277.

[66] Tertullian, as quoted in Henry Chadwick, The Early Church (New York: Penguin Books, 1993), p. 65.

[67] Genesis 41:38.

[68] William Barclay, The Letters to the Galatians and Ephesians (Philadelphia: The Westminster Press, 1976), p. 176.

[69] Plutarch, Moralia, 2.171D.

[70] Seneca, De Ira, 1.15.

[71] The Didache and The Epistle of Barnabas, in The Apostolic Fathers, trans. Kirsopp Lake (Cambridge: Harvard University Press, 1955), 1.319 and 1.402 respectively.

[72] Codex Theodosius, 9.41.1.

[73] Augustine, The City of God Against the Pagans (Cambridge: Harvard University Press, 1963), 5:273.

[74] Recorded in numerous historical texts such as: Fickret Yegul, Baths and Bathing in Classical Antiquity (Cambridge: MIT Press, 1992), p. 34; Edward Gibbon, The History of the Decline and Fall of the Roman Empire (Reprint, London: Penguin Books, 1994), 2.813; Frederic W. Farrar, The Early Days of Christianity (New York: A.L. Burt Publishers, 1882), p. 71; Chris Scarre, Chronicles of the Roman Emperors (New York: Thames and Hudson, 1995), p. 83; etc.

[75] Edward Westermarck, The History of Marriage (New York: Allerton Book company, 1922).

[76] Andrew Guice and Christopher Morgan, "Blair's Gay Vote Dismays Bishops," Sunday Times (London), 21 June 1998, p. 14.

[77] "South Park Hits New Low with Pedophilia, Abortion Themes," American Family Association Journal (August 2000), p. 8.

[78] Statement made at event in the White House's East Room to GLBT leadership on June 28, 2009.

[79] Augustine, City of God, 1.30.

[80] Tertullian, Apology, 3.

[81] Howard S. Levy, Chinese Foot Binding: The History of a Curious Erotic Custom (New York: W. Rauls, 1966), p. 26.

[82] Lin Yutang, My Country and My People (New York: Halcyon House, 1935), p. 168.

[83] Katherine Mayo, Mother India (New York: Blue Ribbon Books, 1927), p. 73; Monica Felton, A Child Widow's Story (New York: Harcourt, Brace, and World, 1966), p. 69; H. G. Rawlinson, India: A Short Cultural History (New York: Frederick A. Praeger, 1952), p. 279.

[84] Dorothy K. Stein, "Women to Burn: Suttee as a Normative Institution," Signs: Journal of Women, Culture and Society (Winter 1978), p. 253.

[85] Rawlinson, p. 279.

Chapter Four

[86] Woodrow Wilson, *The Papers of Woodrow Wilson*, Arthur S. Link, editor (Princeton, New Jersey: Princeton University Press, 1977), Vol. 23, p. 20; "An Address in Denver on the Bible, May 7, 1911."

[87] Russell Kirk, The Roots of American Order (Wilmington, DE: ISI Books, 2008), p. 349.

[88] J. C. Holt, Magna Carta (Cambridge: Cambridge University Press, 1965), p. 317-37.

[89] Martin Luther, An Open Letter to the Christian Nobility.

[90] "Letter to the Princes of Saxony Concerning the Rebellious Spirit," Luther's Works, trans. Bernard Erling, ed. Conrad Bergendoff (Philadelphia: Muhlenberg Press, 1958), 40:58.

[91] Cited by Roland Bainton, Here I Stand: A Life of Martin Luther (Nashville: Abingdon Press, 1978), p. 144.

[92] Thomas Bailey, The American Pageant (Lexington, MA: D.C. Heath, 1975), p. 3.

[93] Published in 1748.

[94] The three branches of government were first outlined by the Old Testament prophet, Isaiah (33:22), "For the Lord is our judge, the Lord is our lawgiver, the Lord is our king; it is he who will save us.

[95] Baron de Montesquieu, The Spirit of Laws, 1748.

[96] Directed by Michael Apted, 2007.

[97] J. Wesley Bready, Lord Shaftesbury (New York: Frank-Maurice, 1927), p. 13.

[98] Ibid., p. 23.

[99] Dale Lee, Family Research Council (FRC, *The Watchman Report*, August 27, 2009).

[100] John Quincy Adams, Letters of John Quincy Adams, to His Son, on the Bible and Its Teachings (Auburn: James M. Alden, 1850), p. 61.

[101] See M. E. Bradford, A Worthy Company: Brief Lives of the Framers of the United States Constitution (Marlborough, N.H.: Plymouth Rock Foundation, 1982), iv-v.

[102] Reports of Committees of the House of Representatives made during the first session of the thirty-third Congress (Washington: A. O. P. Nicholson, 1854), pp. 6-9.

[103] Donald S. Lutz, "The Relative Influence of European Writers on Late Eighteenth Century American Political Thought," American Political Science Review (1984), 189-97.

[104] Montesquieu, The Spirit of Laws (New York: Hafner, 1949, 1962). Sir William Blackstone, Commentaries on the Laws of England.

[105] Ibid., pp. 338-343.

[106] George Washington, The Writings of George Washington, John C. Fitzpatrick, editor (Washington: Government Printing Office, 1932), Vol. 5, p. 245.

[107] William J. Johnson, George Washington the Christian (Millford, MI: Mott Media, 1919, 1976), p. 234-35.

[108] John Adams, The Works of John Adams, Second President of the United States, Charles Francis Adams, ed., Vol. X, (Boston: Little, Brown and Co., 1850, Letter to Thomas Jefferson, June 28, 1813), p. 45.

[109] Richard Hildreth, The History of the United States Six Volumes (New York: Harper Brothers, 1856).

[110] Ibid. "To the Officers of the First Brigade of the Third Division of the Militia of Massachusetts on October, 11, 1798," p. 229.

[111] Patrick Henry, speech in Virginia Convention (Richmond, March 23, 1775).

[112] See David Barton, The Myth of Separation (Aledo, TX: WallBuilder Press, 1991), 25, 158, and M. E. Bradford, The Trumpet Voice of Freedom: Patrick Henry of Virginia (Marlborough, NH: Plymouth Rock Foundation, 1991), iii.

[113] Leo Pfeffer, Church, State and Freedom (Boston: Beacon Press, 1953), 97-98.

[114] John Jay, John Jay: The Winning of the Peace. Unpublished Papers 1780-1784, Richard B. Morris, editor (New York: Harper & Row Publishers, 1980), Vol. II, p. 709.

[115] Henry P. Johnston, ed., The Correspondence and Public Papers of John Jay (NY: Burt Franklin, 1970), Vol. IV, p. 393.

[116] United States Oracle (Portsmouth, NH), May 24, 1800.

[117] Benjamin Rush, Essays, Literary, Moral & Philosophical (Philadelphia: Thomas & Samuel F. Bradford, 1798), p. 112, "A Defense of the Use of the Bible as a School Book."

[118] _____. Letters of Benjamin Rush, L. H. Butterfield, editor (Princeton, NJ: Princeton University Press, 1951), Vol. I, p. 521, to Jeremy Belknap on July 13, 1789.

[119] Noah Webster, History of the United States (New Haven: Durrie & Peck, 1832), p. 339, "Advice to the Young," paragraph 53.

[120] John Eidsmoe, Christianity and the Constitution (Grand Rapids, MI: Baker Book House, 1987), 93.

[121] James Madison, Notes of Debates in the Federal Convention (Athens, OH: Ohio University Press, 1985).

[122] Russell Kirk, The Roots of American Order (Wilmington, DE: ISI Books, 2008), p. 448.

[123] Ibid., p. 363.

Chapter Five

[124] American Presidency Project, "Franklin D. Roosevelt: Address at Dedication of Great Smoky Mountains National Park, September 2nd, 1940" (at http://www.presidency.ucsb.edu/ws/?pid=16002).

[125] Alan Sears, "God in the Public Square," The Arizona Republic (2003).

[126] Ibid., see footnote on p. 360.

[127] Ibid., p. 362.

[128] Joseph M. Dawson, Baptists and the American Republic (Nashville: Broadman Press, 1956), p. 117.

[129] See Leon McBeth, The Baptist Heritage: Four Centuries of Baptist Witness (Nashville: Broadman Press, 1987).

[130] J. M. Carroll, The Trail of Blood (Lexington, KY: Ashland Avenue Baptist Church, 1931), p. 46.

[131] Leon McBeth, The Baptist Heritage: Four Centuries of Baptist Witness (Nashville: Broadman Press, 1987), p. 282.

[132] Abraham Lincoln, Gettysburg Address (1863).

[133] See article by Elihai Braun on the internet at www.jewishvirtuallibrary.org/jsource/biography/Bonhoeffer.

[134] See article by Victor Shepherd at www.victorshepherd.on.ca/Heritage/deitrich.

[135] Arthur C. Cochrane, The Church's Confession Under Hitler (Philadelphia: Westminster Press, 1962), pp. 237-242.

[136] Pastor Martin Niemöller, cir. 1940's.

[137] Robert George, Timothy George, and Chuck Colson, Manhattan Declaration: A Call of Christian Conscience (Drafted October 20, 2009, Released November 20, 2009, www.manhattandeclaration.org).

[138] Sermon given on March 31, 1968 at the National Cathedral in Washington D.C.

Chapter Six

[139] *Journal of the House of the Representatives of the United States of America* (Washington, DC: Cornelius Wendell, 1855), 34th Cong., 1st Sess., p. 354, January 23, 1856; see also: Lorenzo D. Johnson, *Chaplains of the General Government With Objections to their Employment Considered* (New York: Sheldon, Blakeman & Co., 1856), p. 35, quoting from the House Journal, Wednesday, January 23, 1856, and B. F. Morris, *The Christian Life and Character of the Civil Institutions of the United States* (Philadelphia: George W. Childs, 1864), p. 328.

[140] Address to Williams College Alumni, 1871.

[141] Sir William Blackstone, Commentaries on the Laws of England (Chicago: University of Chicago Press, 1979), I:53.

[142] Baptist Press, April 8, 2009.

[143] Baptist Press, June 9, 2009.

Chapter Seven

[144] In Francis Schaeffer, The Complete Works of Francis Schaeffer, Volume 1 (Wheaton, IL: Crossway Books, 1982), p. 11.

[145] Erich Bridges, *What Would Our World be Like without Newspapers?"* (Nashville: Baptist Press, 2009).

[146] Andrea Coombes, *Don't You Dare E-mail This Story* (New York: Wall Street Journal, 2009).

[147] See article in *The Baptist & Reflector* on-line at www.tnbaptist.org.

Chapter Eight

[148] Noah Webster, Letters to a Young Gentleman Commencing His Education to which is subjoined a Brief History of the United States (New Haven: S. Converse, 1823), 18-19.

[149] Noah Webster, <u>Letters to a Young Gentleman Commencing His Education to which is subjoined a Brief History of the United States</u> (New Haven: S. Converse, 1823), 18-19.

[150] See www.pewforum.org, "More Americans Question Religion's Role in Politics."

[151] See WallBuilders web site: http://wallbuilders.com/LIBissuesArticles.asp?id=3930

[152] Charles G. Finney, <u>Lectures on Revivals of Religion</u> (New York: Fleming H. Revell Company, 1868, first published in 1835), Lecture XV, pp. 281-282.

Chapter Nine

[153] Ibid. "To the Officers of the First Brigade of the Third Division of the Militia of Massachusetts on October, 11, 1798," p. 229.

[154] Robert Winthrop, *Addresses and Speeches on Various Occasions* (Boston: Little, Brown & Co., 1852), p. 172 from his "Either by the Bible or the Bayonet."

[155] Paul Coughlin.

[156] *Today's Christian Woman* (Fall 2003).

[157] See www.parentstv.org/ptc/facts/mediafacts.asp

Chapter Ten

[158] Abraham Lincoln, "Proclamation Appointing a National Day of Fasting." March 30, 1867.

[159] Written in a letter to Bishop Mandell Creighton, 1887.

[160] David Fowler, President of the Family Action Council of Tennessee, "Family Action News," Dec. 2008.

[161] Fr. John Flynn, Rome.

Conclusion

[162] John F. Kennedy, "Inaugural Address," January 20, 1961.

[163] Thomas Jefferson, <u>Letter to Danbury Baptist Association of Connecticut</u> (January 1, 1802).

To contact Dr. Shelley for questions or speaking engagements,

write to:

Eight 32 Publishing

P.O. Box 244,
Brentwood TN 37024
www.Eight32Publishing.com

or visit: www.DrDavidShelley.com

LaVergne, TN USA
13 August 2010
193177LV00005B/1/P